Let's face it. Winning and losing in the world of real estate is largely dependent upon your ability to effectively communicate with your clients. Whether in person, over email or direct message, the right words at the right time hold the power to deliver the right results.

Quite often the decision between a client choosing you over another agent depends on your ability to know exactly what to say, when to say it and how to make it count.

This book delivers tactical insight into the power of words and provides tools to empower success-driven individuals to get more of what they want.

This special real estate edition was produced in partnership with Curaytor.

If you want more copies of this book for your team, brokerage or company, email Books@Curaytor.com for bulk pricing and white label options.

All bonus materials mentioned in this book can be downloaded by visiting Curaytor.com/Exactly.

Exactly What to Say for Real Estate Agents is short and to the point—cutting out a lot of the noise from other coaching and training. A sales professional must know how to communicate with modern consumers.

Ilya Rasner, real estate agent, Keller Williams Realty

I feel so much more confident knowing the right words. Not just what to say, but the *right words*.

Susana Murphy, broker owner, ALANTE Real Estate

Of all the coaches, training and a decade's worth of investing, no one ever said to me, "This is the right way to go about it." Then you read this book and it's so obvious. How many listings did I lose as a young agent because I didn't know the right words?

Lisa Sevajian, real estate agent, Compass

EXACTLY WHAT TO SAY

for Real
Estate Agents

EXACTLY

Phil M Jones,
Chris Smith and
Jimmy Mackin

The Magic Words
for Influence
and Impact

WHAT TO SAY

for Real Estate Agents

BOX OF
TRICKS

PAGE
TWO
BOOKS

ISBN 978-1-989603-29-1 (paperback)
ISBN 978-1-989603-30-7 (ebook)

Box of Tricks
www.philmjones.com

Produced by Page Two
www.pagetwo.com

Editing by Jenny Govier
Cover design by Taysia Louie and Mike Mangigian
Interior design by Peter Cocking

The worst time to think about the thing you are going to say is in the moment you are saying it. This book prepares you for nearly every known eventuality and provides you with a fair advantage in almost every conversation.

Foreword

The job of a modern real estate agent is to expertly guide their customers through an important, emotional and complex process.

Some of the people they work with may only buy or sell a home once in their entire life. And for most, it is the largest and most important financial investment they will ever make.

Skill, experience, empathy and an ability to instill confidence in every step of the customer's journey are requirements. When you've done your job to the highest level, your clients will say things like:

- She was honest
- She cared
- She listened
- She was prepared
- She was patient
- She was a complete professional

Think about that last one for a moment. What a powerful word.

Professional.

It's the ultimate compliment.

But what does it actually take to become and be known as a professional?

Ten-time Olympic medal-winner Dara Torres swims 25,000 meters a week to prepare herself for a single 50-meter race. A race that only happens every four years.

Sarah Chang is one of the world's best living violinists.

She was a child prodigy who began playing the violin at the age of four and a half. Sarah practiced several hours a day and toured all over the world nonstop for the next ten years. She took a break at the age of seventeen from playing the violin to enjoy her teenage life.

It lasted one week.

Sarah's talent is undeniable, but it is her dedication to her craft that makes her a living legend.

People often confuse the word dedication with talent.

It took SpaceX six years, hundreds of millions of dollars in capital and countless hours of work from the world's best and brightest minds to prepare the Falcon 1 for its first mission.

It flew for less than sixty seconds.

It wasn't until the fourth attempt that they achieved their goal of launching the Falcon 1 into space and returning it safely to Earth.

Bottom line? Our industry desperately needs new tools and ideas to stay relevant to the modern consumer. The modern consumer is more educated and has more choices than ever before.

Counterintuitively, this has led to more confusion, doubt and frustration in their real estate journey. Therein the opportunity lies.

As a professional communicator, you will have the skills needed to stand out above the competition with your ability to provide clarity and instill confidence.

This is where you add value and justify your fee.

We understand that through the entire customer journey, you are under constant pressure to overcome objections. I'm sure you hear things all the time like:

- I'm just looking right now
- I already have an agent
- I need to talk to my spouse before deciding
- Can you lower your commission?
- My home is worth more than that
- I'm going to wait to list until the spring
- Why hasn't my home sold yet?
- I'm going to sell my house without an agent

In this book, we provide you with thirty-one Magic Words to help you with the most common, critical and difficult conversations you have every day as a real estate agent.

Imagine what it is going to feel like knowing exactly what to say when it matters the most.

That's the feeling you will have by the time you finish reading this book.

Enjoy!

Jimmy Mackin and Chris Smith
Co-founders of Curaytor.com

Getting Started

The very fact that you have picked up this book helps me understand that you are already locked on to the idea that words matter and that your ability to have increased levels of persuasion and influence will allow you to make more of your conversations count.

Throughout my studies of people, human relationships and business interactions, I have been amazed by how some people achieve dramatically different results than others with what seem to be the exact same ingredients.

The real estate industry has people offering what seems to be the exact same thing, often for demonstrably different prices but more importantly with a giant contrast in results. Some agents struggle to find or convert clients, and yet others cannot stop creating more success. Yes, there are factors like attitude, endeavor, experience and good luck that factor into the success metrics of people—but one thing that is also *always* true with every top producer is they know exactly what to say, when to say it and how to make it count.

This truth has been ever-present in each industry I have served, and from as far back as I can remember it has fascinated me that a subtle change of words can make a huge difference to the outcome of a whole conversation. This fascination has fueled my study of the precise language that causes a shift in a person's belief system allowing them to see things differently and thus act differently as a result.

As a professional speaker and trainer I have been packaging my lessons around word choices across the globe and helping people like you have more confidence in conversation by empowering them with what I call "Magic Words."

Magic Words are sets of words that talk straight to the subconscious brain. The subconscious brain is a powerful tool in decision-making because it is preprogrammed through our conditioning to make decisions without overanalyzing them. It works a little like a computer—it has only "yes" and "no" outputs and can never land on a "maybe." It is strong and decisive and moves quickly. Using words that talk straight to the part of the brain that is free from maybes and responds reflexively gives you a fair advantage in conversation and can result in you getting your own way more often.

EXAMPLES

If you are looking for examples of where your subconscious has served you, here are some simple ones:

Controlling your breathing while you sleep.

....

Assisting your routine on a familiar journey.

....

Allowing your attention to be immediately drawn to things you have decided are important.

....

We all rely on our subconscious brain daily to get us through everything that happens without us having to process, compute and take care of every decision all by ourselves. Think of the subconscious brain as nothing more than the little voice inside your head.

In this book, you will learn many of these Magic Words, and also some useful frameworks and thought processes with precise examples that relate to your daily interactions in the world of real estate. The goal is to not only help you know exactly what to say, but also to provide you with the principles behind these word choices and allow you the freedom to craft your own examples.

These words are tried, tested and proven to deliver results in your industry, and when applied properly can be a powerful tool in your negotiations.

This book is about far more than just Magic Words, however. As you work through each section, you will receive powerful insight into what makes people tick and learn how simple changes that you can apply instantly can make your life so much easier. Yes, the advice is aimed at increasing your success helping more people buy and sell homes, but every principle discussed is easily transferable into almost every area of life, to help you become more persuasive and influential and have a bigger impact in all that you do.

My advice is to have a notebook and pen with you when you read. Look to create your own examples as you work through each section. Then make the decision to try them for yourself as soon as possible, getting more comfortable and confident each time you do. Everything I share may sound simple, but simple does not necessarily mean easy. Get comfortable being uncomfortable and know that if you want to change your results, you may need to change your actions.

Change your *words*. Change your *world*.

Before we dive into the words and their examples, it's important that you understand a fundamental truth about negotiation.

Who is the person in control of a conversation?

If you did not yet realize what happened there, that was an action of the very lesson being shared. It is the person that is *asking* the questions that is in control of the conversations.

Many of the examples in this book are simply prefacers, frames and lead-ins to allow you to control more of your conversations by improving your ability to ask better questions.

Why are questions important?

Well...

Questions start Conversations

Conversations build Relationships

Relationships create Opportunities

Opportunities lead to Decisions

If you want to increase the quality and quantity of decisions in your life you have to start by asking better questions.

1

I'm Not Sure If It's for You, But

One of the most common reasons I hear from people as to why they fail to introduce themselves, a property or their service to others is the fact that they are fearful of rejection.

It was for this reason that I figured the best place to start is with a set of Magic Words you can use to introduce just about anything to just about anybody, at just about any point in time, that is completely rejection-free. The words in question are, "I'm not sure if it's for you, but . . ."

It fascinates me that we face rejection in dozens of other areas in our lives yet, in our business we can be so afraid they may say no that we fail to even ask. This could be the very reason that your friend or neighbor lists with a stranger, your work colleague secures a new qualified buyer or a family member refinances their home without even speaking with you about who your trusted local lender is.

If you do not ask, then you do not get.

Let's take a moment to understand how this simple structure works.

Opening a statement with the words, "I'm not sure if it's for you," causes the listener's subconscious brain to hear, "There's no pressure here." By suggesting that they may not be interested, you naturally increase their intrigue; their curiosity is spiked as they wonder what "it" is, and this spike in curiosity makes them want to learn more. Additionally, it fires an internal driver that tells them a decision needs to be made, and this softer approach ensures this decision doesn't feel pressured, and is theirs to make.

When you say to somebody, "I'm not sure if it's for you, but…," the little voice inside your listener's head hears, "You might want to look at this."

The real magic, though, is delivered through the final three-letter word of this sequence, a word that typically should be avoided in all conversations: the word "but."

Imagine receiving a comment from a past employer that started with the words, "You know that you're a really valuable member of the team. We love everything that you do here, but some things need to change." What's the only part you would remember? I am guessing the part that you would focus on most is everything that follows "but." The word "but" negates everything that was said prior, so when you say to somebody, "I'm not sure if it's for you, but…," what the little voice inside your listener's head hears is, "You might want to look at this."

EXAMPLES

Here are a few examples to help you in your daily routine:

I'm not sure if it's for you, but when the time is right I would be delighted to help you get the best price for your home.

I'm not sure if it's for you, but there is an open house on Saturday, and you're welcome to join us.

I'm not sure if it's for you, but there is a new listing coming up next week that could be a good fit.

I'm not sure if it's for you, but I have a great relationship with the local building managers and could help you secure a great unit.

I'm not sure if it's for you, but I have a great resource who you should speak with if you are thinking of refinancing.

I'm not sure if it's for you, but I checked out the Zestimate on your home and found a few errors.

This rejection-free approach creates a simple outcome.

One of two things happens: your listener leans in and asks for more information because they are personally interested, or, in the very, very worst-case scenario, they say they will give it some thought, whilst memory-pegging the conversation to recall at a later date.

2
Who Do You Know?

The trouble with real estate is the fact that almost everybody is a prospect. We all need to live somewhere and renting, buying, selling, leasing or investing are things that appear as requirements in most people's lives.

This fact can easily result in a new Realtor becoming annoying to almost everyone they meet, by projecting their ability to help in *every* conversation.

Instead, shift the direct ask away from the person you are speaking with and toward a third person who you currently do not know. This way it becomes instantly easier to create opportunities from your daily interactions, without being pushy.

Instead of asking if people need a Realtor, think of the circumstances somebody may find themselves in where an agent could add value to them. Scenarios that spring into my mind are situations like:

- Moving to the area
- Moving to a new area
- Upsizing or downsizing
- Considering home improvements
- Completing home improvements
- Considering investing in real estate

EXAMPLES

Here are a few examples to help you in your daily routine:

Who do you know that is considering moving to the area?

Who do you know that is thinking of moving to the suburbs/city?

Who do you know that may be looking for more/less space?

Who do you know that could be interested in a valuation of their current home?

Who do you know that has talked about potentially investing in real estate?

Who do you know that could be interested in this three-bedroom townhome?

You may notice in these examples that each question is fueled in possibility and not certainty. Using words like "thinking about," "could be," "may be," "might" and "considering" deliver more fluidity to the conversation and allow the other person to further explore their memory and see how they could open a door for you.

There is another added bonus with this approach. You may just stumble directly onto an opportunity without directly asking for it.

If you ask a friend, family member or co-worker, "Who do you know that may be looking for more space?" You could quite easily discover the very person they are thinking of is themselves, and your polite ask, aimed at helping to solve a challenge for a third person gives them the confidence to volunteer themselves.

Who do you know that you should be asking more "who do you know" questions of?

3
Open-Minded

If you were to ask a room of a thousand people whether they considered themselves open-minded, I am sure at least nine hundred of them would raise their hands.

Just about everybody in the land thinks of themselves as meeting this criterion, and it's pretty easy to understand why.

When the alternative is being considered "closed-minded," it becomes easy to use this thought process to better package your idea. Knowing that people like to see themselves as open-minded, you can easily give yourself a fair advantage within your conversations. When introducing a brand-new idea to a stranger, friend, prospect or team member, including the words, "open-minded" as part of a question creates an incentive for them to want to be agreeable to your ask. The simple preface "How open-minded are you?" followed up with your suggestion naturally makes your idea significantly more attractive. This preface shifts you from having fifty-fifty odds of them agreeing with you to odds of ninety-ten in your favor. Everybody wants to be open-minded.

EXAMPLES

Here are a few examples of the words in practice:

How open-minded would you be to working with an experienced local agent to help you sell your home?

_____

Would you be open-minded to reducing your asking price?

_____

How open-minded are you to looking at something that could be perfect but a little over your budget?

_____

Would you be open-minded to considering some alternative neighborhoods?

_____

How open-minded are you to working with a trusted local lender to get this approved?

_____

How open-minded are you to listing your home while the market is strong?

_____

How open-minded are you to listing your property during the winter when there are fewer homes for sale but still a lot of serious buyers?

_____

Each of these options makes it very difficult for the other person to entirely reject your idea, and it at least makes them feel obligated to explore the possibility. It seems like you are giving them a choice, when really you are heavily weighting the only option you are giving them. Put simply, "How open-minded are you to at least trying it?"

When introducing a new idea, start with, "How open-minded are you?" This will naturally attract people toward the very thing that you'd like them to support. Everybody wants to be open-minded.

4
Opening-Fact-Question

This is not a set of Magic Words, instead it is a framework that promptly, professionally and with permission, launches you into the heart of many an important conversation.

Too many conversations can be clunky to get started, and the small talk is uncomfortable and off-putting for everyone involved.

Simplifying a universal route into almost any conversation has you prepared to start from a position of confidence and avoid that nervous dance of an awkward opening.

The framework follows three simple steps.

1   A polite **opening**
2   A mutually agreeable **fact**
3   An easy to answer **question**

These steps keep you in full control of the conversation and get to the purpose quickly. The opening lets them know they are speaking with a real person and delivers them context for the conversation, the fact provides an agreeable framework for the purpose of the conversation and once the question is answered, you have clear permission to proceed.

EXAMPLES

Here are a few examples to help you in different scenarios:

Responding to an inquiry on your listing

Hi it's (insert name) calling from (insert agency)

You recently showed some interest in (insert property address)

Is this the only property you are interested in?

Outreach to a For Sale by Owner (FSBO)/ expired listing

Hi it's (insert name) calling from (insert agency)

You may not know me, but I have sold a lot of properties in your area and I have noticed you were looking to sell (insert property address)

Is this property still available?

Responding to a listing inquiry

Hi it's (insert name) calling from (insert agency)

I understand you are thinking of selling your home and are interested in how we may be able to help.

What is it that prompted you to contact us specifically?

Requesting an online review

Hi it's (insert name) calling from (insert agency)

Now that you have successfully moved into your new home, I was hoping you may be in a position to help me out.

Would you be open-minded to leaving a review online about your experience working with me?

The applications for this three-step formula are truly abundant and my challenge to you is to think specifically about your next conversation and how you can use it to launch straight into the discussion you are planning to have.

5
What Is Your Experience?

All too often you can find yourself in a conversation where you are being asked questions about yourself, your service and your pricing—all without the context of understanding where the other person is coming from.

Earlier you learned that it is the person who is asking the questions that is in control of the conversation. It can, however, be all too easy to find yourself on the back-foot with an unqualified interrogation forcing you to embarrassingly justify your existence.

You can manage this circumstance proactively by simply meeting the other person exactly where they are, and anchoring your discussion based on *their* level of experience.

Instead of being challenged by questions like,

- How much is your commission?
- What is my house worth?
- Will I get approved?

You can lead a conversation by skillfully asking a question that creates a frame for their opinion to be encased in and reaffirms your expertise in the conversation. You do this by prefacing your question with the words "What is your experience…?" and this leaves them obligated to share any historic references they are basing their questions on.

EXAMPLES

Examples you could use in the real world are…

What is your experience with selling houses?

What is your experience with buying a new home?

What is your experience with applying for a mortgage?

What is your experience with working with a professional Realtor?

What's your experience with timing the market?

Calmly and kindly asking questions like this immediately reverses the control of the conversation and helps you discover where they are coming from.

It's possible that you uncover a distinct lack of experience that translates to a fear or anxiety in them. It is at this point that you get the opportunity to help reassure them that this is exactly what you are there to help them with. You are looking for them to literally value *your* experience.

6

How Important Is It?

Buying and selling real estate is rarely something that happens without compromise appearing on at least one side of a transaction.

Understanding this can greatly assist the managing of expectations and reaching a compromise if the boundaries are agreed on ahead of time.

Boundaries can be crafted by testing the beliefs of others with questions that challenge their thinking and have them start to quantify their responses. Moving people from a list of likes and dislikes and adding further dimensions to their preferences gives you levers and anchors to help others reach compromises and make smarter decisions.

You can efficiently achieve these boundaries by asking questions that start with the words "How important is it?" You soon learn what the essentials are and what their "nice to haves" are.

EXAMPLES

Examples you could use in the real world are...

How important is it that you sell your home quickly?

How important is it that you have the extra bedroom?

How important is it that you achieve that price?

How important is it that you move before the holidays?

How important is it that we secure this specific property?

How important is it to you to find the perfect home for sale before you decide you to list your current home?

When you ask these questions, you are bringing purpose to any advice you may have to give and are using their reasons and not yours to justify your point of view.

Their answers to these questions allow you to amplify your advice by using their words and not yours. If someone said they need to move before the summer, you could say "because you said that you need to move by the summer, I recommend we list at the lower price with the goal of attracting increased early interest."

A further technique to build on this same tool is to create further clarity on their boundaries by applying a sliding scale to their list of preferences.

Imagine adding the preface "on a scale of one to ten, with ten being essential and one being irrelevant," to your "how important is it?" questions and you learn very quickly the areas in which you can work toward a compromise.

7
What Do You Understand?

How often do you find yourself in a conversation that quickly becomes a debate because you are speaking with someone who thinks they know best and perhaps even wishes to lecture you on their opinions?

To influence others who are confident of their position, you must move the other person's position from one of certainty to one of doubt.

Typically people try to create this position of uncertainty through directly challenging the other person's opinion and perhaps even entering into an argument. I am sure you have had moments when you have been frustrated by someone's inability to understand what you are saying and flustered that you cannot overcome their precon- ceptions. This can happen regularly when you are trying to introduce your unique value, an alternative property to consider or a curve ball to the plan, and the "I know best" mentality of others can become difficult to overcome.

The best way to overcome the "I know best" mentality of many people is to **question the knowledge on which the other person's opinion was founded.**

I feel certain that you want to stop people from arguing with you, so this situation could regularly result in you backing down, walking away and failing to get your point across. For an opinion to have merit, however, it really should be founded on some form of knowledge. The best way to overcome this kind of conflict is not to win the argument; instead, you must question the knowledge on which the other person's opinion was founded. The goal is to turn the situation into one in which the other person admits that their opinion was based on insufficient evidence, while still retaining the ability for them to save face in the conversation. It is the power in the preface, "What do you understand about…?" or "What do you know about…?" that softly threatens their knowledge base and forces them to share the reference on which their argument is based. Often this results in them realizing their strong opinion was unfounded.

EXAMPLES

Examples you could use in the real world are…

What do you understand about us, our business and the way we do things differently?

·····································

What do you understand about the pitfalls of working with a part-time or inexperienced agent?"

·····································

What do you understand about the home buying and selling process?

·····································

What do you understand about the new amenities and infrastructure planned in (insert neighborhood)?

·····································

What do you understand about the ways we determine a price at which to market your home?

·····································

These questions allow the other person to realize their opinion is perhaps incorrect, and they can quickly become far more receptive to change.

The worst that can happen is that you learn the precise basis of their argument and can then position your point in contrast to it. Use words like this to challenge others with confidence and avoid arguments that always end with losers since, regardless of who the loser is, you are unlikely to leave with your desired result. Either every-body wins, or everybody loses.

8
How Would You Feel If?

Perhaps the most overused word in the business world is "motivation," yet still, when I have asked my audiences at events to share with me what the word actually means, all I see in response are blank faces.

It is the meaning of this word that creates the true base for understanding all areas of negotiation, influence and persuasion, and exploring it further will help you get more from yourself *and* others.

Put simply, understanding this word would mean that you could probably get just about anybody to do just about anything.

The word motivation derives from two very common words forced together. The first part of the word, the "motiv-" part, is derived from the Latin word "motivus," the modern-day translation of which is "motive." Another word for motive is "reason." The "-ation" part of the word is derived from the word "action," and if somebody is going to take action, they are going to do something or move. This means that a very simple definition of motivation is "a reason to move" or "a reason to do."

Now ask yourself this: would it be fair to say that if the reason were big enough, you could get just about anybody to do just about anything?

If you want people to do things that typically they do not want to do, first you need to find an honest reason that is big enough. Understanding what reasons are big enough means you have to understand how people are motivated. People are motivated by one of two things: either avoiding a loss or acquiring a potential gain. They either want to go toward the light, the good thing that they are looking for, or they want to get away from the thing that could potentially hurt them. In the world of real estate, focus is often based on the positive side of a transaction, and yet, the real world tells us that people will work far harder to avoid a potential loss than they will to achieve a potential gain.

The real world tells us that people will work far harder to avoid a potential loss than they will to achieve a potential gain.

Some of the people, *some* of the time will move to become more comfortable.

More of the people, *more* of the time will move when they are uncomfortable.

The greater a contrast you can create between where somebody does not want to be and where they hope to be, the more likely you are to get people to move. Understanding what motivation really is, a contrast in circumstances that creates movement, and coupling this with my next point, gives you real context for this set of Magic Words.

Consider this. Do people base their decisions on emotion or logic? The true answer to that question is, in fact, both; it is just that the decision is always made for emotive reasons first. Something needs to feel right, before it can ever make sense.

I am sure you have stepped away from a listing presentation or a showing confused about why the other person did not move forward, and thought to yourself, "I don't know why they don't do it. It just makes sense for them to do it."

If you are trying to win the argument based on your idea making sense, you are calling out to the wrong set of reasons. People make decisions based on what feels right first. If you can make it feel right, the logical argument can then confirm that feeling.

Understanding the meaning of motivation and the fact that emotions drive decisions is the foundation for this set of Magic Words. It is all brought together in another preface to a question. By introducing a future conditional scenario with the words, "How would you feel if. . .?" you allow the other person to time travel to that moment and imagine the emotions that would be triggered at that point. Choosing moments that trigger both positive and negative emotions allows you to create a set of circumstances worth changing for. It also helps to prepare others to accept your ideas on how to help them achieve success or avoid a potential loss.

EXAMPLES

Examples might be something like...

How would you feel if your home didn't sell quickly?

How would you feel if someone else beat you to your dream home?

How would you feel if we created a bidding war?

How would you feel if we could make that happen for you?

How would you feel if you lost your buyer?

How would you feel if six months from now your home was still on the market?

An evolution on this is demonstrated in the form of creating hypothetical scenarios to get the person with whom you are speaking to consider someone else's point of view.

"How do you think the buyer (or seller) would feel if…"

Creating these conditional future scenarios using the words, "How would you feel if…?" gets people to feel their future and gives them a reason to move either toward the good news or away from the bad news. Remember, the greater the contrast, the more likely you are to get that someone to move.

9
Just Imagine

Did you know that every decision any human makes is made at least twice? The decision is first made in your mind hypothetically before it is ever made in reality.

In fact, for a conscious decision to become a reality, you must have first at least imagined yourself doing it. Have you ever been in a situation in which you have said, or even just mouthed, these words back to somebody else: "I just couldn't see myself doing that"?

It is a literal thing. If you cannot see yourself doing something, the chances of you doing it are slim to none. People make decisions based on the images they see in their minds, so if you can place pictures in people's minds, then you can use the results of those images to influence their decisions.

Creating pictures in the minds of others is done by telling stories. We remember as children many a good story that started with the words, "Once upon a time…" When we heard those words, we knew it was time to kick back, enjoy the moment and embrace our imagination while someone used words to paint a world for us to jump into. It would be really tough to engage adults with that same powerful preface, so you need some Magic Words that create the same picturesque outcome. When you hear the words, "Just imagine," the subconscious brain kicks a switch and opens up the image viewer, and it cannot help but picture the very scenario you are creating.

Previously, you learned about **away** motivation and **toward** motivation. You can apply those exact same rules to how you complete your "just imagine" scenarios and help drive people to "see themselves" in scenarios you would like them to move toward or stay away from.

Here are some examples: **EXAMPLES**

Just imagine how life will be once you have moved into your new place.

Just imagine losing out on this property to a higher bidder.

Just imagine the look on your kids' faces when they see this backyard.

Just imagine this remaining on the market for another six months.

Just imagine the girls having their own rooms.

Just imagine yourself in their shoes.

Just imagine what it's going to feel like when a buyer walks in here and the house is impeccably staged.

Allowing the power within the other person's creative mind to build your case for you will always save you guessing at their motivators, and can create a more vivid reality than anything you could possibly describe. Let them do the hard work. Imagine saying to your client following an over-asking price offer, "Just imagine what you could do with the extra money" or, "Just imagine the memories you will make in your new home," or, "Just imagine how good your car will look in the driveway." As you make those statements, they will see the picture of that very thing happening. Now that they have seen the thing, the chances of their belief in it becoming a reality go through the roof. I mean, just imagine the difference these words and this book are going to make for you and your business.

Creating pictures in the minds of others is done by telling stories. When you hear "Just imagine," the brain pictures the very scenario you are creating.

10
How Certain Are You?

For a negotiation to happen, something that must be present is an element of uncertainty. This means that to start a discussion in which you are looking to influence the thoughts and beliefs of some- one else, a great place to start would be to gain a commitment that they are less than certain of their current thoughts.

Creating this commitment to uncertainty is achieved by presenting them with an open question to quantify a possible closed response. It is a fabulous tool for helping to prevent somebody from making a potential expensive decision and avoiding your "I told you so" moment appearing later.

Think of the scenarios in which a false certainty can result in a potential client possibly committing to a decision that you feel is less than ideal for them.

- They are going to list with a friend or relative who has recently received their licence
- They are rejecting a good offer in anticipation of a better one
- They are refusing to stage their property as they don't believe it is worth it
- They are failing to see the value in your marketing efforts
- They are planning to market their home themselves or through a lower-cost option

In each of these situations, you hold the ability to question their judgment in their potential decision and open the possibility of an alternative course of action.

EXAMPLES

Examples you could use in the real world are…

How certain are you that they have the experience to get the best outcome for you?

_____

How certain are you that this is not the best offer you will receive in this market?

_____

How certain are you that the effort in staging won't be worth it?

_____

How certain are you that you will get a high quantity of interest without progressive online marketing?

_____

How certain are you that a lower cost option will leave you with more money in your pocket overall?

_____

How certain are you that selling your home without a Realtor will save you money?

_____

By challenging their position and asking them to commit to being "certain" of their point of view, you can often open their mind to considering the bigger picture, and it can allow you to position an alternative point of view.

When it is time to position what you are suggesting as an alternative, you can increase your influence by shifting your thoughts to a more powerful, third party response, and you can create even more confidence in the new idea.

"**The reason** our clients keep coming back to us time and time again is because we have a proven track record in maximizing sales prices by gaining increased levels of interest, as well as having a highly experienced team to efficiently navigate the transaction from offers through to closing."

11
Could It Be Possible?

Building on our lessons around certainty, the flip side is that of possibility. In the same way that "uncertainty" can create opportunity, exploring what is possible achieves a very similar outcome.

You see, the alternative to certainty, we have already learned, is doubt. Doubt is your friend when negotiating, as creating a feeling of doubt in someone else opens the door to create a new reality, something new of which they can feel certain.

To shift someone else's belief, we can borrow a line of questioning from the courtroom and use a preface that allows people to quickly see something from another angle and, in turn, promptly change their opinion.

The words "could it be possible" give us the instant ability to make suggestions about alternative realities and educate the other person on something they may have overlooked through their own decision-making process. It is challenging, rejection free, without aggression and laced in curiosity.

It becomes a very natural way to follow your "How certain are you?" questions as it presents the movement you are looking for immediately after they have admitted a lack of certainty.

EXAMPLES

Examples you could use in the real world are…

Could it be possible that working with an experienced agent would be a more appropriate solution for your current circumstances?

Could it be possible that you receive no better offers and we find ourselves with an expired listing?

Could it be possible that the other agent is suggesting your home is worth more purely to secure the listing?

Could it be possible that spending a little time and money on the staging might add thousands to the sale price?

Could it be possible that choosing us would be a better option for you?

....

Could it be possible that I could get you more money for your home with fewer headaches and less stress than if you were to do everything yourself?

....

Could it be possible that these words allow you to get more clients to see the sense in working with you and not make the mistakes so many others do?

Because you have phrased your recommendation in the form of a question it allows them the freedom to move toward your ideas, without needing to admit their previous idea was wrong. Creating this freedom in a conversation to allow others to let go of past truths is a skill that requires practice if you want to be able to use it intuitively.

12
Help Me Understand

Confusion can easily lead to confrontation and confrontation can quickly escalate to an argument. We know that arguing with clients and prospects is a bad idea, it's just that sometimes you don't see eye to eye and you would really like to see the world through their lens.

Instead of creating a conflict or telling somebody that you do not understand them, make your lack of understanding all your own fault.

By taking full responsibility for your possible ignorance you can invite the other person to justify their thoughts by educating you about how they crafted them.

This is achieved by replacing the typical "tell me" preface with the words "Help me understand…" Softening the ask removes the threat and without argument in the tonality of the question, you can again get to the evidence on which their opinion is founded. What you achieve is a shift of responsibility and you openly grant permission to the other person to teach you something.

Being vulnerable in this nature is a mature and elegant way of helping someone else to perhaps see for themselves that they might not be making the smartest decision.

EXAMPLES

Examples you could use in the real world are...

Help me understand why you are thinking of listing with the other agent?

....

Help me understand why you don't want to make any upgrades before selling?

....

Help me understand what you have read that makes you think that?

....

Help me understand your thoughts about the current market conditions?

....

Help me understand the benefits of selling without an agent?

....

Help me understand what would cause you to want to sell your home within the next ninety days?

....

When you ask these questions, the other person is instantly and politely asked to justify their position and often realizes for themselves that what they previously presented as a fact was nothing more than an uneducated opinion.

Be brave enough to approach an unreasonable response with a very reasonable question, and courteously craft an outcome that is back in your favor in no time at all.

13

When Would Be a Good Time?

This simple set of words helps us overcome one of the biggest challenges faced when trying to get people to get back to you or even reconsider your offer.

My guess is that you have regularly heard sellers say that they have not decided if they want to go to market yet, or have had buyers put off making the time to visit properties in a new area or even received a stack of interest at an open house and struggled to find an appropriate way of following up.

By using the preface, "When would be a good time to…?" you prompt the other person to subconsciously assume that there will be a good time and that "no" is no longer an option. This assumption acknowledges that there will be a time when this can definitely fit into their schedule and that it is just a case of confirming the specific time and date. It is this kind of direct question that prevents people from telling you that they do not have the time and, as a result, keeps you in control of the conversation and prevents the need for pushy and desperate follow up.

EXAMPLES

Examples for you to use include...

When would be a good time for you to take a look at the area and what is available?

When would be a good time to get your home photographed?

When would be a good time for your home to be sold by?

When would be a good time to speak next?

We just sold a property down the street from your home. **When would be a good time** for you to review your home's new value?

The preface "When would be a good time to…?" prompts the other person to assume that there will be a good time and that "no" is not an option.

In all of these scenarios, please be certain that when you gain a reply, you work to schedule the precise next point of contact in order to keep control of the conversation in your hands.

When you do get around to having the next conversation, be wary of the fact that some time has gone by since you last spoke and these changes could certainly impact their behavior and thoughts. This is easily accounted for by asking a "what's changed with you since…?" question and, providing you are not presented with an answer that introduces something that would affect what you had previously discussed, you can now proceed as if all previous information is still true.

14

I'm Guessing You Haven't Got Around To

Sticking to the theme of following up with people, I thought I'd share some words that you can use in those scenarios in which you are fearful of contacting the other person because you think they have not done the thing you would like them to do.

You know the times when you have sent over some details or they have said they needed to consult with someone else, and now you need to make contact to take the next step?

When you are fearful that somebody has not done something, instead of asking them how that thing went, you may want to start the conversation slightly differently.

Open the conversation by allowing the other person to save face, but also preventing them from using any of the excuses you think they might use. This leaves them with nowhere to go in the conversation other than where you would like them to go. The reason they cannot use the excuses is because you have been bold enough to start the conversation in a way that suggests they were about to use the very excuse they had prepared: by prefacing your question with, "I'm guessing you haven't got around to…"

Imagine you are making a telephone call to someone who said they needed to meet with other agents before making a decision.

If you ask, "I'm guessing you haven't got around to speaking with the other agents yet?" it now becomes impossible for them to use that excuse. They respond in one of two ways: either they feel proud that they have done what they had promised, or they are embarrassed that they haven't and make a new promise to put right that fact.

Other examples could be... **EXAMPLES**

I'm guessing you haven't got around to looking over the documents yet?

I'm guessing you haven't got around to setting a date yet?

I'm guessing you haven't got around to making a decision yet?

I'm guessing you haven't got around to making those repairs you wanted to do before you listed your home?

By pushing for the negative scenario, you get people to rise to the positive or to tell you how they are going to fix the thing they said they were going to do.

By using the words you are fearful they may give you back in the other direction, you create a scenario that completely disarms them. If you say to somebody, "I'm guessing you haven't got around to making a decision on this yet," and they say, "No, you're right. We're still thinking about it," you can open up the negotiation. If, instead, they say, "No, we have, and we've made a decision," you can say, "Great, when are we ready to get started?"

By pushing for the negative scenario, you get them to rise to the positive or to tell you how they are going to fix the thing they said they were going to do, because most people are people of their word and feel pretty bad when they are called out for it.

15
You Have
Three Options

People hate to feel manipulated and nearly always want to feel like they made the final decision. When someone needs help deciding, using these words can help narrow their gaze, reduce their choices and make it easier for them to pick.

The words, "As I see it, you have three options," help the other person through the decision-making process and allow you to appear impartial in doing so.

These words are perfect for an indecisive seller, an unrealistic buyer and even a landlord who has false expectations on his rental prices.

You are simply presenting them with their options, yet you now have the opportunity to display them in a way that favors your preferred choice. The rhythm of three makes for easy listening for the other person, and by leaving your preferred choice until the end, you easily build the value of that option and load the choices so your preferred outcome stands out as a clear favorite.

For sure, we could play with several examples. In fact, we could probably think of dozens that relate to the world of real estate. Let's start with just one for a nervous, first-time seller.

Imagine you have a first-time seller who is nervous about taking her home to the market.

Start by making a statement that sets the scene for the real-life scenario. That statement might run something like this:

"So, you are ready to move into something new, have collected an abundance of fond memories here, made some improvements to the property and you are looking to secure over $300,000 for the sale to allow you to purchase the home you have seen in the new neighborhood before someone else beats you to it. You are interested and intrigued about the low-priced listings advertised elsewhere and are questioning the value of working with a professional, local Realtor."

Following this scene-setter you might say…

"As I see it, you have three options. First, you could list with a flat-fee listing service, which would mean tackling much of the administrative tasks yourself and risking not getting the eyeballs you need on your listing to achieve the price you need. Second, you could do absolutely nothing, stay exactly where you are right now, not follow through with a move and let someone else purchase your dream home instead of you.

"Or third, you could commit to working with me, have us professionally present your property to the market, maximize the interest in it, secure you multiple offers and manage the entire process start to finish for you and even help negotiate your offer on your next home.

"Of those three options, what's going to be easier for you?" Finishing with another set of Magic Words means they have to favor one of those options.

"What's going to be easier for you?" means that the laborious self-service option is off the table. Since staying put was already off the table, the only option they have left is the easy one—the one you want them to pick; the one you left to the end and stacked in your favor because you made that the path of least resistance. So, start with, "You have three options," finish with, "What's going to be easier for you?" and watch people effortlessly pick the choice that previously they were finding so difficult to make.

16
Two Types of People

In real estate, a large part of the job is the responsibility of helping people make up their minds.

To me, the primary job description of all sales professionals is to be "decision catalysts" in the lives of their clients and prospects, yet still the job can be more simply described as "professional mind-maker-upper."

There are many people who do a great job of getting people interested in something, yet it is the final moment of helping people decide that creates the action that drives results. That is the tough part.

Help people to choose by removing some of the choices and creating easy options. Decisions become easier when the choices are polarizing. Fully renovated or fixer-upper, colonial style or new construction, city center or rural retreat—all become simpler decisions than the broader alternative. Your goal is to create a statement that presents choice and then to allow the other person to pick.

Asking people to decide for themselves who they are with the Magic Words "two types of people" prompts a near-instant decision. The second someone hears, "There are two types of people in this world," the little voice in their head immediately wonders which one they are, and they wait with bated breath to hear the choices.

EXAMPLES

Now your role is to deliver them two choices and make one of them stand out as the easy option. Here are just a few examples:

There are two types of people in this world: those who know a good offer when they see it, and those who look back thinking what could have been.

There are two types of people in this world: those who try to save money in the short term and those who value the experience of investing in a professional.

There are two types of people in this world: those who resist change in favor of nostalgia and those who move with the times and create a better future.

You should be able to see the pattern in the examples and understand how the options are clearly stacked in favor of the decision you would like them to pick.

Something for you to think about as a reader is that there are two types of people in this world: those who read books like this and do nothing and those who put what they read into practice and enjoy immediate results.

17

I Bet You're a Bit Like Me

This set of words is possibly one of my favorites because it can help just about anybody agree to just about anything. It is even more powerful in a conversation with a stranger than it is with somebody you already know.

When you are talking to a stranger, the conversation needs to move easily and without friction, which means it typically follows the path of least resistance.

If you use this preface ahead of a scenario you would like people to believe to be true, expect them to agree with you wholeheartedly, quickly and easily. Prefacing a statement with the Magic Words, "I bet you're a bit like me," quite often results in the other person comfortably agreeing with what you are saying, providing that you are reasonable.

This serves as a wonderful tool to help gather evidence to use in building your later recommendations. My experience has taught me that many clients, prospects and people in general are not always completely honest. Getting them to provide evidence that supports your objective makes it harder for them to disagree with you. You can use this set of words to help avoid many common objections by gaining full agreement with something they may otherwise have tried to use as a future excuse.

The Magic Words "I bet you're a bit like me" often result in **the other person comfortably agreeing with you.**

EXAMPLES

Imagine you are fearful of someone objecting to working with you. Early in the conversation you could say something like...

I bet you're a bit like me: when I am selling something I want to get the best possible price with the least amount of effort.

I bet you're a bit like me: you know the difference between price and value and make decisions looking at the bigger picture.

I bet you're a bit like me: you're always juggling to get everything done and love it when you have someone who just takes care of things for you.

I bet you're a bit like me: when I am selling something I want to get the best possible price with the least amount of headaches and stress.

Slipping those kinds of statements into early conversations while holding eye contact with the other person, and just watch them nod back at you.

When they do, this means they know that you know they agree with those concepts. This makes it an awful lot harder for them to tell you they do not see the benefit in working with you. Please note that success when selling anything has far more to do with destroying the option of "no" than it does with embellishing the option of "yes."

18
If...Then

Our speech patterns, listening patterns and, in turn, belief systems are all preprogrammed and hardwired into us throughout our childhood—

so much so that the repetitive patterns of words we receive through to our adolescence create habits, systems inside of our belief systems, that we lean on in order to support our personal decision-making process.

An example of this is a simple pattern of speech that appeared a lot in your youth, and its impact can be too easily overlooked. Adults delivered many conditional statements to us when we were children, such as . . .

If you don't eat all your dinner, **then** you're not going to get any dessert.

—

If you don't study hard at school, **then** you're not going to get into the college or job you're hoping for.

—

If you don't tidy your room, **then** you're going to be grounded for the weekend.

—

EXAMPLES

When they made conditional statements like these to you, chances are that you believed them. These statements hold power over our beliefs and actions.

As a consequence, creating a scenario using the preface "if" and adding a second scenario with the preface "then" means that people are highly likely to believe the outcome.

If you decide to work with me, **then** I promise you won't be disappointed.

If you put your home on the market now, **then** you could be closed before the end of the year.

If you decide to list with them, **then** you won't have access to our marketing services.

If you follow through with the staging, **then** you are likely to sell for more money *and* sell more quickly.

If I can show you the top three reasons why your home didn't sell, **then** would you be willing to meet to discuss me representing you?

By creating these "if … then" sandwiches, you can position guaranteed outcomes that are very difficult not to believe. If you are prepared to give this a try, then I am certain you will see the results as early as the first day you try it.

19
Would It Help If?

At points of indecision it is often nothing more than a subtle nudge of positivity that can promptly turn a "maybe" into a "yes." The biggest thing we can do to demonstrate our value and show our worth is to genuinely be helpful to others. Better than that is to present an offer of help that is almost impossible to refuse.

It is the moment in which they accept your offer of help that frees up any friction that may have existed and was holding them back from choosing you. This method is unlikely to make a difference to someone who sees no value in you or your services, instead it can make a radical difference to someone stuck in "maybe."

Phrasing your offer of help in the form of a question makes it entirely conditional and presents a hypothetical door for them to step through. "Would it help if…?" is a tool for you to dangle a piece of bait without forcing or pushing it on them. It keeps you in control and allows you the benefit of only following through with your offer of help if it makes a difference to them making their decision.

EXAMPLES

Examples you could use in the real world are...

Would it help if you could speak with some past clients and learn about their experience working with us?

Would it help if you knew that the only way I get paid is when we close on a sale at an amount you are happy with?

Would it help if I could pick you up and drive you between the properties?

Would it help if you only paid the full commission if we secure a buyer at or over the asking price?

Would it help if I introduced you to a trusted local lender who is familiar with the area?

Would it help if I broke down the common missteps sellers make when listing their home with a discount broker?

Presenting an olive branch of "help" creates a natural bridge to ease them into the next stage and shows them your desire to work with them and your willingness to put in effort on their behalf.

Choosing the right offer of help becomes your only challenge, but remember, making the offer in the form of a question does not leave you obligated to follow through on your offer and it also means that if you miss with your first offer, you can create alternatives until you reach a level of commitment.

20
Don't Worry

What I love best about this next set of simple words is the power they have on people who are nervous, apprehensive or showing signs of concern.

You know when you can see and feel the anxiety in somebody, when they are uncertain about what to do next or perhaps even fearful. These two Magic Words provide a mild, instant relief, and it is common to even "see" the relieved tension in their physiology.

Say the words, "Don't worry," and the tension just pours out of them as they become more relaxed. Just two words that, when said confidently and calmly, create an outcome that is the equivalent of the expression "Phew!"—that little sigh that comes out as they start to feel in control.

This is particularly useful in high-stress scenarios, when confronted with someone who is panicked or just to comfortably put someone at ease. The minute somebody is indecisive, hold your posture, stay relaxed and give them the feeling that you have this under control and can help them navigate the next step.

EXAMPLES

Examples include...

Don't worry. You're bound to be nervous right now. This is your home and you want to do the right thing.

Don't worry, I know you don't know what to do right now, but that's what I'm here for. I'm here to help you through this process and overcome all the hurdles as they crop up along the way.

Don't worry. This happens sometimes and it's one of the many reasons that you work with an experienced Realtor. Let me make some calls and we can work on a plan for what to do next.

So, don't worry if you're wondering how you're going to make all these new word choices stick. They will come in time, and you will have soon mastered it, getting a little better from one conversation to the next.

"Don't worry" is particularly useful in high-stress scenarios, when confronted with someone who is panicked—it puts people at ease.

21
Most People

These two words, which contain just ten letters, are possibly responsible for more of my negotiating success than any other single strategy I have employed in my businesses.

Indecision is often a major factor that stops people from moving forward with you, standing in the way of progress. The Magic Words "Most people..." hold the power to help jump people out of procrastination into decisiveness.

Understanding why these words hold so much power is dependent upon your knowledge of two basic psychological principles.

First, people take great confidence from the fact that people like them have made a decision before them and that the decision worked out just fine.

We like to follow other people and the experience others have had in a situation can go a long way in influencing our own decisions. This is why when choosing a restaurant you are possibly more likely to believe the reviews of forty-seven strangers on Yelp than you are the recommendation of your mother-in-law.

Secondly, people don't like being told what to do, as that can appear rude. They may not like being told what to do, but they do like to know what to do. Also, people don't like telling people what to do, but people do like to be led. This may sound like a bit of a riddle, but in which lies the point.

You often find yourself in situations where you want to deliver direct advice and tell people what to do. But you can't tell people what to do, because that is rude. But, they want to know what to do without being told what to do, because they are longing to be led.

Take this fact and couple it with the first lesson around safety in numbers and next time you want to tell someone what to do, instead, explain what "most people" would do.

When you introduce people to what most people would do in their situation, it is likely to trigger their subconscious brain to say, "Aha, I'm most people, so if that is what most people would do, then perhaps that is what I should do too."

When you tell people what most people would do, their brain says, **"I'm most people, so perhaps that is what I should do too."**

EXAMPLES

The examples for this are endless:

Most people who list with me sell over their asking price.

Most people find that the first offer they receive is typically the best one.

Most people in your circumstances would ensure their home is presented at its best if they wanted to reach for the highest possible price.

What **most people** would do with inspection concerns is make a contingency for the buyer.

Most people want to make a bunch of last-minute repairs to their home but that's not always necessary.

Try arguing with each of these points and see how much they can be used to strengthen your point of view. In fact, most people put the words "most people" into some of their daily conversations, and most of those people see an immediate positive effect on their influence.

Most people put the words "most people" into their daily conversations, and most of those people see an immediate positive effect.

22
The Good News

Now is the time for us to talk about how you can turn around all that negative energy–the negative energy that comes with the territory of negotiating complex and emotional transactions.

These words provide you with a tool to spin a negative into a positive using a technique called labeling.

The moment you apply a label to something, and that label is not contested, it is then assumed true by all parties.

It is the acceptance of this new label that creates the ability to change the direction of a conversation with minimal effort and move it toward a more positive outcome.

Using the Magic Words, "The good news is…" as a preface to your chosen point ensures that the recipient has to accept the label you have attached to it. This optimistic spin can help you face negativity in your life, prevents you from ending up in a self-sabotaging conversation of blame and pity and helps you start to build in a new direction.

If someone presents an offer that gets rejected, then you can respond with, "Look, the good news is that we have learned that there is no deal to be done on this property and you have not paid more than you needed to."

If you are recruiting someone who is unsure whether they have the skills that are required in order to make it as a real estate agent, you could say, "The good news is that we have comprehensive training you can complete at your own pace to give you all the skills you need to be successful in this industry."

What about when somebody is resisting changing from their last agent but says they want more success? You could respond with, "The good news is that you already know what working with them is like, so what is the harm in trying this?"

By prefacing things with, "The good news is…," you cause people to face forward with optimism, zap any negative energy out of the conversation and create a positive next step.

By prefacing things with, "The good news is . . . ," you cause people to face forward with optimism and zap any negative energy out of the conversation.

You can use this same principle with two more words when faced with people who give excuses or complain about the activity not reaping the results they hoped.

When somebody gives you an excuse, they expect you to push back and argue the point or sympathize with them. Next time somebody complains about something, respond by saying, "That's great." When somebody says, "I don't like any of the offers," say, "That's great, we are learning more about the market and where you may need to compromise" and watch how they look at you differently. You have changed the way that they think and made every new question or concern progressive toward the actual goal.

By bringing more positivity to situations with, "The good news is…" and responding with, "That's great," you soon start shifting the balance in people's thoughts and allow them to question themselves toward a better outcome and behavior.

EXAMPLE

The good news is that we now know what the key reasons why buyers aren't making an offer and we can address them head on.

23 What Happens Next

Let's apply some context that happens in many of your listing presentations.

You have created an opportunity, got a red-hot prospect, been out to their property, shown them how you can help them and walked them through your entire presentation, and now you are at the point where they have nodded and smiled all the way through everything you've presented to them.

They have all the facts, you want them to commit, but following all of this relationship building and imparting of knowledge, the conversation grinds to a stop with nobody leading the actual decision.

This happens far too often, and it is a product of people being so fearful of being seen as pushy or controlling that they fail to finish the job they started. It can be all too easy to leave the decision-making up to other people and hope that they will make the right choice, but without your help, often others make no decision at all and everyone loses out.

In these consultative discussions, it is your responsibility to lead the conversation, and following the sharing of the required information, your role is to move it toward a close.

You need to let them know what happens next, so the Magic Words to help are precisely that: "What happens next is…" This is a perfect way of linking all of the information they need to make a decision, the information you provided when you presented to them, and bringing them through to the completion that needs to follow. So, what you do is create a scene. You do not ask them what they would like to do; you just tell them what happens next.

"What happens next is that we are going to take a few moments, complete some of your personal details so we can start the process of bringing your home to market.

"Then we need to schedule another meeting for us to ensure your home is presented well for showings and take photographs so that potential buyers see it looking its best. Throughout the entire process you have my complete support and attention to ensure that every question is answered and we achieve the best results for you. In terms of photographing your home, would midweek or the weekend work best for you?"

Finishing this process with a question that is effortless to answer is the key to gaining a rapid response and a positive outcome.

In the example just discussed, you should see how, just by asking them that simple question at the end, the second they respond with their preference, it means they are moving forward with your proposal.

You could comfortably ask any type of question to close your scenario. The easier the question is to answer, the easier you gain your decision. Having a concise and constructive "what happens next" conversation will mean that you successfully close far more conversations in the first meeting and make more happen in the moments that you have with people.

It is your responsibility to lead the conversation, and following the sharing of the required information, your role is to move it toward a close.

The easier the question is to answer, the easier you gain your decision.

What happens next is I'm going to pull comps of homes near your property that have sold to get a better idea of how the market trends have impacted your value over the last few months. Then I'm going to call you back to review all the details.

24
What Makes You Say That?

Objections are a common part of everyday life. We face indecision from others in our personal and professional lives and quite often find ourselves having to accept another person's idea.

These conversations can become confrontational, so to avoid argument, the majority of people are happy to let go of their goal in favor of an easy life.

To overcome an objection, you must first understand what an objection really is. There is always the possibility that an objection is an alternative to saying, "No thank you," or a way of pushing the decision away for another day. However, it is always a shift in control of the conversation, and the second any objection is raised, the other person seizes power and you are obliged to respond to their wishes.

You already know that success in negotiating is all about maintaining control in a conversation, and the person in control is always the person who is asking the questions. By treating every objection you face as nothing more than a question, you can quickly regain control of the conversation by asking a question in return.

In a business setting, common objections include…

EXAMPLES

I haven't got the time.

....

It's the wrong time.

....

I want to shop around.

....

It is outside of my budget.

....

I need to speak to somebody else before I make a decision about this.

....

Success in negotiating is all about maintaining control in a conversation, and **the person in control is always the person who is asking the questions.**

The worst thing that you could do when such an objection is raised is to respond with your counter argument and make statements that disprove their current opinion. Instead, you can tackle each of these common objections effectively by being inquisitive about them and asking a question in the opposite direction.

Of course, you could develop unique and precise questions to challenge every objection you are faced with. Alternatively, you can lean on the one set of Magic Words that has served in millions of similar scenarios: "What makes you say that?"

Here are a few examples: **EXAMPLES**

The customer says, "I need to speak to somebody else before I make a decision about this." You say, **"What makes you say that?"**

The customer says, "Really, that is outside of my budget." You say, **"What makes you say that?"**

The customer says, "I'm really not sure we need to do an open house." You say, **"What makes you say that?"**

The customer says, "I'm not willing to pay a commission." You say, **"What makes you say that?"**

This shift of control now leaves the other person obligated to give an answer and fill in the gaps in their previous statement.

It prevents you from making prejudgments or entering into an argument, and it allows you to better understand their point of view before recommending a next thought or action.

What you are asking them to do is to explain themselves properly. The words, "What makes you say that?" mean they now have to take responsibility and explain what they really mean. An alternative to the "What makes you say that...?" question is a personal favorite of mine and is not in fact a question, instead it is just a single word, phrased as a question.

When an objection is raised that sounds to you as more like an excuse, or a stall, a choice you now have is the ability to respond inquisitively with the word "Really?"

Say for example that somebody suggests that they have decided to market their property without an agent...

You would simply respond, "Really?"

And not add a single further word, allowing the pause to serve as your friend and possibly create a sense of uncertainty around their decision. Remember that uncertainty and doubt are gifts to your ability to reopen a negotiation.

25
Before You Make Up Your Mind

Moving somebody from a "no" to a "yes" is nearly impossible. Before you can move someone to full agreement, your first action is to move them to a position of "maybe."

When you find yourself in a position in which the other person is leaning toward not choosing your idea, you can quickly move them back in your direction by prefacing your next action with another set of Magic Words: "Before you make up your mind..."

EXAMPLES

Here are some examples of how you can use these words to keep the conversation alive:

Look, **before you make up your mind,** let's make sure we've looked at all the facts.

Before you make up your mind, why don't we just run through the details one more time so you can know what it is that you are saying no to?

Before you make up your mind, wouldn't it make sense to look at what similar properties have actually sold for?

Before you make up your mind about who you're going to hire, let me prepare a marketing plan to show you how I'm going to sell your home for more money than the average agent.

These simple examples can often move people from a position of "no" and allow the negotiation to continue by making them look at it from a different perspective.

It is this shift in vantage point that then allows you to add alternative information to support your idea and increase your influence over their decision.

26
If I Can, Will You?

Have you ever been in one of those scenarios in which your prospect or client pushes back with reasons as to why they cannot do the thing you would like them to do?

Perhaps they are looking for you to make a change from your standard terms or they would like you to lower your commission.

Likewise, you have probably experienced a friend or family member making excuses about why they cannot make it to an event or celebration.

These situations are created when the other person delivers an external condition that is affecting their ability to move forward with your suggestion. They have removed themselves from the process and abdicated responsibility to something out of their control.

You have the power in these situations to isolate this condition and remove the barrier by responding with a powerful question that eliminates their argument. This is achieved by using the question structure, "If I can…, then will you…?"

Imagine that you want a friend to join you for a night out next Friday. Your friend says the reason they cannot join you is because their car is in for repair and public transit does not run that late. You could eliminate this challenge with the question,

"If I can pick you up and drop you off at home, then can you be ready at seven pm?"

The same principle can be used when someone is looking for you to reduce your price in line with a competitive offer.

"If I can match that price for you, then would you be happy to commit to working with me?"

In both of these scenarios, you are still not obligated to meet the condition presented, but you are in control of what happens next. You may receive further reasons and honesty from the other person that prevents you moving forward, or you may find that you gain their agreement. With their agreement to the condition, you can now present your best option to them and will be far more likely to reach your desired outcome.

You have the power in these situations to remove the barrier by responding with a powerful question that eliminates the other person's argument.

27
Just One More Thing

When selling products and services it is not uncommon to have something known as an upsell—inviting your customer to purchase more at the point of transaction.

A practice that is far less common is the idea of a downsell. A downsell involves working on achieving a lesser objective if you fail to meet your primary objective in a conversation.

Perhaps you went in looking to secure a listing; a downsell could be an introduction to a friend looking for a rental. Or perhaps you took a potential buyer to a showing that was not for them; the downsell could be an introduction to your mortgage broker.

This set of Magic Words allows you to create that opportunity on your way out of a conversation. Instead of leaving with nothing, you use these words for a further attempt of leaving with at least something. I first learned the power of this technique while watching crime dramas on TV at my grandparents' house as a child. These shows introduced me to possibly the greatest negotiator I have ever met, the television detective Columbo, who was famous for a precise set of words.

He would quiz his suspect, deliver a comprehensive interrogation gathering all the information he could, and then turn to leave.

Just when the suspect was sure they had gotten away with things, Columbo would turn back to them and, with his finger pointed upward, would say, "Oh, just one more thing." It was in this moment, when the suspect's guard was down, that he could ask his next question and receive the key information that was often missing—the clue that would lead him to solve the crime.

This is real estate and not high-stakes detective work, but the principles translate in exactly the same way.

An example that would likely resonate with you would be the almost countless times that you have taken someone out on a number of showings, but failed to find something for them to move forward on.

They have shown signs that they have found value in working with you, but on this occasion, it seems as though no business is to be done. You thank them for their time, and it looks as though you are to conclude the meeting. At this point you could create a Columbo moment and turn back to them with the words, "Just one more thing." When they think that they have gotten away with not committing to anything, you introduce a simple idea, something that is really easy for them to commit to, and bring them into your world with a far smaller decision than you had previously asked for.

EXAMPLES

Examples of things you could add with a Columbo moment include …

Asking them to provide you an online review or share their experience on social media.

Asking them to commit to a Comparative Market Analysis of their existing home.

Inviting them to your next open house.

Introducing them to a preferred partner of yours.

Asking them to introduce you to others.

Asking them a question that allows for your next conversation.

146

Using these moments and the Magic Words "Just one more thing" keeps the conversation alive and can help you avoid leaving with nothing.

EXAMPLE

Just one more thing, I'm going to reach out later today with a link to review my services.

28
A Favor

Success in life and business is rarely achieved without the support of others. Asking others to support your own objectives has the power to significantly increase the chances of you achieving them.

I am sure you have had many scenarios in which you have longed for someone else to do something that makes your life a little easier, that opens a door for you or provides you with the information you need to make the progress you would like.

As we approach the end of this book, perhaps you could do me a small favor?

Think for a second about how you feel about me asking you that direct question, "Could you do me a small favor?" I am pretty sure that in that split-second moment, you felt okay with the ask and perhaps even agreeable to take action.

This is a simple and powerful set of Magic Words that you can use to get somebody to agree to do just about anything before they even know what the thing is. The request of a favor almost always gains a unanimous agreement from the recipient, and the worst response possible is still a conditional yes, like, "Depends what it is."

The reason this precise ask holds such power, is almost exclusively achieved because of its timing. The reason you felt okay with my earlier ask, is likely that you have already received value from what you have previously read, and have prejudged any ask that I may have for you as reasonable. The timing of this ask is best positioned after you have delivered significant amounts of value to the other person.

Examples that come to mind for me where your value exchange is high and your ability to ask is enabled would be situations like:

- Securing a great offer for your client
- Helping a prospect find their dream home
- Negotiating a great compromise
- Introducing a valuable third party
- Running a successful open house
- Taking the time to show someone a new area

At each of these moments you have the ability to ask for something extra that could benefit you with the words, "Could you do me a small favor?"

Think of the things that you could ask people to do following their agreement to the favor you are asking of them. I am sure your mind is boggled by the dozens of things you could add to your list of wants and the people who could help you with them. In this book I want to illustrate how much can be done with a powerful change of words. We can explore the application of these Magic Words using the topic of referrals.

If you are ever unsure of what to ask, your one default option can always be a referral into a potential new opportunity. Growing a new client base from your existing happy clients is a solid strategy for business growth, yet it is often not implemented at all. I believe that there are three main reasons people fail to ask others for referrals:

1   They are too lazy and cannot be bothered.
2   They do not know *when* to ask.
3   They do not know *how* to ask.

Let's consider the first reason—being too lazy to ask. Mostly it would relate to the people who do not read business books, attend training or take their personal development seriously. This clearly does not describe you, so I guess we should consider the other two reasons.

When it comes to the timing, we have already considered multiple scenarios where an ask can be well timed and there are certainly dozens more. Considering all the prior examples of "good times," they will all have one thing in common—the other person is happy with what you have delivered for them. When people are happy with what you have done for them, there are some simple words that nearly always feature: they express their happiness with the words "Thank you." Instead of just allowing these words to stroke your ego and trigger feelings of pride and self-worth, also consider how another person must be feeling if they are showing gratitude toward you.

An expression of gratitude comes from a feeling of indebtedness. Put simply, when they say thank you, it is because they feel they owe you something. The best time to ask for someone's help is in the very moment when they feel indebted to you. All this means is, the next time you hear the words "Thank you" from your client or prospect, use that as your cue to ask for "a favor."

People say thank you when they feel they owe you something. This is the best time to ask for someone's help.

Now that you have the timing, let's next determine how to ask.

So, they have said, "Thank you," which provides you with your cue to ask your first question: "You couldn't do me a small favor, could you?" This simple question gains an almost certain agreeable response and gives you instant permission to continue with the rest of your request. You can then go on to say,

"You wouldn't happen to know..."

(This throws down a challenge, which makes people want to prove you wrong.)

"...just one person..."

(Just one, because it's reasonable and seems a simple ask, and they're more likely to think of someone by name.)

"...someone who, just like you..."

(This has the person narrowing down the options and gives you more of the right prospects, plus it pays a subtle compliment.)

"...would benefit from..."

And then emphasize the specific benefit or positive experience they have just thanked you for.

Then... *shut up!*

When they have thought of somebody, you need to know where to go next. You will probably see in their body language when they have thought of somebody. At this point, say, "Don't worry. I'm not looking for their details right now, but who was it that you were thinking of?"

This automatically takes the pressure off, and the "but" helps them to recall only the final part of the sentence. Find out then when they're next likely to see the person they thought of.

"You couldn't do me a further favor, could you?" (I mean, they said yes the first time.) "Next time you see Karen, could you share with her a little bit about how it was doing business with me and see if she's perhaps open-minded about taking a phone call from me to see if I can help her in the same way I helped you?"

Your client will almost certainly agree.

"Would it be okay if I gave you a call next week to find out how the chat with Karen went?"

They will most likely, again, be agreeable. You will then call when you said you would and ask, "I'm guessing you didn't get around to speaking to Karen?"

As a person of their word, either they will proudly say that they have spoken to Karen, or they will be embarrassed and tell you how they will go on to complete the introduction.

The magic in this, the crazy irony, is that you slow the process down, but you speed up the outcome and end up having conversations with people who expect your call, look forward to hearing from you and are grateful for the introduction. It provides you with qualified future customers who already have third-party experience with your offerings, as well as permission to make contact. I would take that over a name and number any day of the week.

It is now time to do yourself a favor and look at all the things you can be asking of others, gaining their commitment before they even know what that thing is.

29
As Promised

Have you ever started a phone call with somebody using the words, "Is now a good time to talk?" If so, please *stop it*.

Those words served a purpose at a point in history when a phone ringing was a rare occurrence. Phones were connected to walls by cords and a telephone conversation was viewed as a formal means of conversation. In modern times, more often than not, if it's an inconvenient time to have a conversation, the recipient will let the call divert to voicemail or just ring out.

The reason that people still use this opening is because they are trying to be polite and only proceed with the discussion if it is with the permission of the other person. My lens though, is that regardless of circumstances, a call that needs to start with these words is almost always unexpected by the recipient and as a result of which is an interruption to their day. Starting with an interruption is unlikely to garner the result you desire, often meets resistance and adds to the fear they may have of you being pushy.

Instead of being pushy, our goal is being able to punctuate the opening of your conversation with the Magic Words "As promised."

When you introduce your actions or behaviors, inclusive of these words, you are weighting your efforts and showing the other person you are working on their behalf and acting in their interest, this then fuels a feeling of indebtedness and is highly likely to have them thanking you for your efforts as opposed to feeling like you are being pushy.

Creating the ability to open conversations in this way means that you must schedule and confirm your promise ahead of time to allow you to be able to communicate your fulfilment of this.

Put simply, this means saying what you are going to do and gaining agreement before you do it.

Examples would be:

- Scheduling a specific time for a phone call
- Agreeing to take some further pictures or a video of a potential property
- Putting together pros and cons of potential alternatives for your buyer
- Creating a list of comparable properties that have sold against which to measure pricing
- Making an introduction to a preferred vendor

Sometimes you can make agreements for these actions verbally, and alternatively you can use technology to support you and entirely change the frame of your next conversation.

Even with an inquiry for a listing, you could respond with an email or text message that confirms that you will be phoning them that evening at a specific time and then use that email as your permission to open your conversation with the words, "I am just calling as promised" in place of the dated "Is now a good time to talk?"

Examples you could use in the real world are…

As promised, here are the contact details for a handful of people we have helped relocate to the neighborhood over the last six months.

Attached you will find the research on sales of similar properties **as promised.**

As promised, I spoke personally with the home inspector and let him know your concerns.

Here are the extra photos and video **as promised.**

As promised, I have the home value report prepared for your home and I'm ready to send it over to you now.

Each of these examples is almost guaranteed to create a grateful response from the other person and is a practical reminder of the value that you deliver.

30
Just Out of Curiosity

There is one objection that people give in response to ideas that has always frustrated me. This objection is, "I just need some time to think about it."

I am not saying that people should feel rushed into decisions. It's just that my experience tells me this statement rarely means they are heading away to do a detailed analysis of their decision. They are just pushing their decision away to another day. It's not an objection, but instead a stall.

Apply some context to this, and consider that you have spent time responding to an inquiry, visiting a prospect in their home, getting to know them and listening to their plans and challenges. You then provide them with a detailed set of recommendations to help them achieve their desired outcome, in which they only pay you if you follow through on your promise, and in return they provide this vague response that doesn't help anybody in the discussion to reach closure.

My concern is that this seems less than fair. I believe that if you have delivered your part correctly, then the other person at least owes you a little more transparency regarding their thoughts.

On receipt of this reply, I have often found myself wanting to shout, "What is it that you want to think about?" I knew that if they could open up their thoughts to me, then I could probably help. The trouble was, I knew I couldn't really ask that because it would seem rude or obnoxious. So instead, I hear people in this situation say things like, "It's okay, no pressure; we are ready when you are ready," and walk away from the opportunity hoping that time will fix it.

This frustration has meant that I have had to find a way of getting a real answer from people and discover how to ask direct questions without sounding rude or obnoxious. What I want from their response is not a guaranteed commitment, but honesty in the discussion so that we both know what the true obstacles are.

My frustrations and explorations into this led me to discover that if I preface one of these direct questions with a certain set of Magic Words, I could change rude and obnoxious into soft and fluffy. By finding a reason or purpose for my direct question and gaining permission to ask it, I instantly shift control of the conversation to me. The words I use to do this are, "Just out of curiosity," and they can be used as the perfect preface to many a direct question.

Examples include ... **EXAMPLES**

Just out of curiosity, what is it specifically you need some time to think about?

_____

Just out of curiosity, what needs to happen for you to make a decision about this?

_____

Just out of curiosity, what's stopping you from moving forward with this right now?

_____

Just out of curiosity, do you know why the average FSBO sells for significantly less than a home represented by a Realtor?

_____

In each of these examples, what is imperative is that you remain quiet following your question. Silence becomes your friend; you must not prejudge their answer or put words in their mouth. They now know they need to give you a proper answer, and one of two things will happen.

Asking big, brave questions is exactly what you need to do to become a professional mind-maker-upper.

Thing number one is that maybe twelve seconds goes by. (This will feel like three weeks.) They will then come back with a real, honest answer, and you can work with that transparency. The second option would be that the time runs on longer. This is good news. Bite your tongue, sit on your hands, do nothing. Let the time go by. During this elongated pause they are hunting for an excuse and often realize they do not really have one. They then respond with things like, "You know what, you're right. There isn't anything to think about," or, "There is nothing that needs to happen," or, "There is nothing stopping me." It's the very fact that you were prepared to ask them the question they were not yet prepared to ask themselves that empowers them to make a decision you both know was right for them in the first place. Asking big, brave questions is exactly what you need to do to move from being just like everybody else to becoming a professional mind-maker-upper.

31
Simple Swaps

By now you should be more than convinced that a simple change in words can create a profound change in outcomes.

Sometimes it is the subtlest of changes, and here are two precise examples of a unique variance in how you phrase a question that moves you from self-sabotaging your success to amplifying your chances instead.

The first example came to me when I was trying to prevent a giant mistake that I see many people make when they reach the end of a presentation.

Following many a presentation, the question people reach for is, "Do you have any questions?" Asking this creates the subconscious suggestion that the other person should have questions, and if they don't, it leads them to wondering what they have missed and creates indecision that was perhaps not previously present. The result is that you then hear objections like "I need some time to think about it" and the conversation parts without any future action being agreed upon.

A simple change of wording moves this from pushing the conversation out of your control to steering it toward a controlled decision. Swap the phrase, "Do you have any questions?" with the improved, "What questions do you have for me?" and your common answer should now be "no questions" which in turn means they have made a decision and you can invite them to take the next step. The only alternative would be that if they did have questions you would receive them at this moment and, answering their immediate reservations, should also create the clarity they need to move forward.

Either way, you are far closer to a decision, and you avoid the dreaded, "I need some time to think about it."

That was the first simple example, but I promised two for one in this section. This next change is so simple and so profound, yet the mistake that prompts me to share this tip with you is ever present in this industry.

It was from my own experience as a home buyer and my further research for this edition of the book that I became more and more confused as to why people would keep asking a very specific question at open houses that would provide the easiest way for me to shrug off an agent. The typical early question was "Are you working with an agent?" and in my opinion, this question is as useful as the retail sales associate asking, "Can I help you?" It prompts an almost certain response that closes the conversation and makes further communication now uncomfortable for all parties.

Instead we should ask questions that lead the discussion toward the outcome we desire and not away from it. If the retail sales associate had asked the quetion "Where have you traveled from today?" could it be possible they would have gotten an easier answer and learned more about the visitor? The exact same process translates to an open house, and the answer to this question contains a wealth of knowledge that gives you context as to the intent of their visit. Better still, it sets you up to ask the next question in a way that supports your objective instead of destroying it. Swap the closed question "Are you working with an agent?" to the assumptive and more open question "Who is your Realtor?" and watch how many more of your visitors admit to not being locked into anyone specific, and those who are already committed now share more with you about their position, empowering you with increased information for you to help them in their decision-making process.

The same principle applies to swapping "Can I have your email address?" to "What is the best email address at which to reach you?"—one creates resistance and the other is friction free.

Both of these examples demonstrate how changing a couple of words can make all the difference in the results you get from your conversations.

Changing a couple of words can make all the difference in the results you get from your conversations.

Exactly What To Say for Real Estate Agents: Field Guide

Now that you know what the Magic Words are and why they are so powerful, you are undoubtedly going to want to apply them in the most common, critical and difficult situations you face as a real estate agent.

That is exactly why we built this Field Guide for you, so that you could quickly come back to it over and over again while you prospect for new customers (lead generation), attempt to close those customers (lead conversion), take care of those customers (customer service) and then turn those customers into more opportunities (referrals).

Each entry in the Field Guide has three simple components:

1 Common types of people you work with or moments you face
2 Difficult objections and situations that come up
3 Exactly what to say when they do

Keeping this Field Guide by your side empowers you with the right words at the right time for the right people.

Want this Field Guide as videos and audio files? Email Chris@Curaytor.com.

Field Guide

Types + Moments	Objections + Situations	Magic Words
Expired	I'm going to relist with the same agent again	**How important is it** that the next time you list your property, it actually sells for a price you're happy with?
Expired	I'm not ready to relist	**Most people** in your situation feel the same way. They believe their home is never going to sell, but I can prove to you that we can sell your home for a price you'll be happy with.
Expired	I'm not willing to lower my asking price	**How would you feel if** six months from now your home was still on the market?
Expired	A lot of people have already called me and said the exact same thing	I understand. I'm sure lots of agents are promising you that they can sell your home for more money and less time than your previous agent. **Help me understand** why you think your home didn't sell the first time you listed it?

Types + Moments	Objections + Situations	Magic Words
FSBO	I don't want to be tied down with a listing agreement	**The good news is** that I have a simple cancellation policy with my agreement. If you're not happy with my services, you can cancel the agreement.
FSBO	Bring me a buyer and we can talk	**The good news is** I work with a lot of serious buyers. When would you like me to bring one over?
FSBO	I'm not willing to pay commission	**Would it help if** you only paid commission if we secure a buyer at or above the asking price?
FSBO	I'm going to list with a discount broker	**What's your experience** working with a full-service agent?
FSBO	I can sell my house without you	**Just out of curiosity**, do you know why the average consumer sells their own home for significantly less than when represented by a professional real estate agent?
FSBO	I'm not in a hurry	If I can prove to you that I will generate serious buyers for your home, **would you be open-minded to** listing with me down the road?

Types + Moments	Objections + Situations	Magic Words
Circle Prospecting	A home was just listed near theirs	**I'm not sure if it's for you**, but your neighbor is selling their home and I can put together a report on how their sale will impact your home's value.
Circle Prospecting	You have an upcoming open house	I have an open house coming up in your area. **Who do you know** that might like living next to you?
Circle Prospecting	A notable home just hit the market	I just found a property near your home that's going to sell very quickly. **I'm not sure if it's for you**, but I can get you all the details just in case you have a friend who's actively looking to buy.
Zillow Make Me Move	I'm not in a hurry	**Would you be open-minded to** selling your home sooner if we find the perfect buyer this month?
Zillow Make Me Move	I'm just going to use Zillow	**What's your experience with** selling your home without guidance from a real estate agent?
Zillow Make Me Move	I already have interest	**Just out of curiosity**, did any of them put in an offer?

Types + Moments	Objections + Situations	Magic Words
Forced Registration	How did you get my information?	I'm following up, **as promised**, because you registered on our website.
Forced Registration	I'm just browsing	**I'm not sure if they're for you**, but I have a few homes that are similar to the one you inquired about that I could share with you.
Forced Registration	Unresponsive	(Voicemail) **I'm not sure if it's for you**, but I have access to homes in your area before they get listed in the MLS.
Facebook Buyer Lead	· I'm just browsing	**I'm not sure if they're for you**, but I have a few homes that are similar to the one you inquired about that I could share with you.
Facebook Buyer Lead	Unresponsive	(Voicemail) **I'm guessing you haven't gotten around to** reviewing the list of properties I sent over. Text me a good time for us to chat and review your options.
Google PPC Lead	I'm just browsing	**Don't worry!** I work with clients during all stages of the buying process. Some of whom are many years out and just browsing, and some of whom want to buy a house today.

Types + Moments	Objections + Situations	Magic Words
Google PPC Lead	Unresponsive	(Voicemail) **If** I could I find the perfect home for you, **then** would you be interested in having a quick chat? Please text me a good time for us to chat and review your options.
iBuyer	I'm going to buy a home without a real estate agent	**What makes you say that?**
Zillow Lead	I just want to know if the home is still for sale	I can look that up for you. **The good news is**, either way, I also have access to homes that aren't on Zillow and I can prepare a list of those for you.
Zillow Lead	I want to work directly with the listing agent	**How certain are you** that the listing agent will have your best interests in mind?
Zillow Lead	I don't need a buyer's agent yet	**What do you know** about submitting a winning offer in a competitive market?
Zillow Lead	I'm just browsing	**Would it help if** I sent you listings that aren't on Zillow while you browse?
Zillow Lead	I'm waiting for the perfect home	That's smart. **The good news is** I can help you find it.
Zillow	Zillow says my home is worth $X	**Tell me what you know** about how their Zestimates are calculated.

Types + Moments	Objections + Situations	Magic Words
Open House	I'm already working with an agent	**Just out of curiosity**, who is your agent?
Open House	I don't want to pay commission	**Tell me what you understand** about how our commission works.
Open House	Invite your prospects to your open house	**I'm not sure if it's for you**, but there is an open house on Saturday, and you're welcome to join us.
Seller Lead	I just want to know how much my home is worth	I've prepared a new home value report for you. **When would be a good time** for you to review it?
Seller Lead	I'm not looking to sell right now	**Would you be open-minded** to finding out how much your home is on track to be worth when you are ready to sell?
Seller Lead	I didn't think a real estate agent would be contacting me	**Don't worry!** I'm only reaching out to make sure the home value report you requested is accurate.
Seller Lead	If the market is going up, why shouldn't I wait to sell later?	**What do you know** about timing the market?
Seller Lead	Zillow says my home is worth $X	**What do you know** about the difference between a Zestimate and a CMA?

Types + Moments	Objections + Situations	Magic Words
Seller Lead	I'm just going to list my home with a discount broker	**Before you make up your mind**, can I send you an in-depth report about how much I think your home will get?
Seller Lead	I don't think I can afford to buy a new home	**Would it help if** I could show you how your mortgage payment could actually be less than what you pay for rent?
Seller Lead	I'm going to interview a few more agents	**Help me understand** what you're looking for in the perfect agent.
Seller Lead	Touch base with me in a few weeks	**Would it help if** in the meantime I sent you a list of homes that recently sold near yours?
Seller Lead	I'm going to list my house without a real estate agent	**Before you make up your mind**, let me send you a breakdown of how I think I could actually make you more money than if you sold it by yourself—including my fees.
Seller Lead	My relative/friend is a real estate agent	**Could it be possible** that mixing family and business is a bad idea?
Pre-Appointment	I'm going to be meeting with a few other real estate agents	**When would be a good time** to connect after you've had a chance to meet with all the other agents you're interviewing?

Types + Moments	Objections + Situations	Magic Words
Pre-Appointment	Before we meet, how much do you charge?	I charge X%. **The good news is** you don't pay any out-of-pocket cost or commissions until your home is sold. I will explain everything in detail when we meet.
Listing Appointment	I'm going to be interviewing other real estate agents	**Just out of curiosity**, what would you consider to be the top three criteria you're looking for in that perfect agent?
Listing Appointment	I want to list my home at $X (way above market value)	I understand that you think your home is worth $X, but **how open-minded are you** to pricing it lower than that if it could create a bidding war?
Listing Appointment	Are you willing to lower your commission?	**What do you know** about how real estate commission works?
Listing Appointment (iBuyer)	My friend just sold their home without an agent	**Could it be possible** that your friend left money on the table by not hiring a professional?
Listing Appointment	We're going to have to think about it	If I can show you some data about the difference between selling your home now and waiting six months, then **would that help** you make a better decision?

Types + Moments	Objections + Situations	Magic Words
Listing Appointment	I need to talk to my spouse	**I bet you're a bit like me** and you run every important decision by your spouse. What questions do you think they will have that I can answer for you now?
Listing Appointment	We're going to use the same agent who helped us last time	I can prepare a plan to help you sell your home and, at the very least, you'll have something to compare to theirs. **Would you be open-minded** to exploring all your options before you make your final decision?
Listing Appointment	Will you offer me a guarantee?	**If** you're willing to follow my advice and list your home for the right price, **then** it will sell.
Listing Appointment	I'm not willing to stage my home	**Would you be open-minded** to staging if you knew your home would sell for more because of it?
Listing Appointment	I want to find my next house before I sell this one	**Don't worry!** I've helped many people who have been in the exact same position you are in right now. That's why you hire an expert. I'll help guide you through this entire process.
Listing Appointment	I want to wait until the busy season	There may be fewer homes for sale right now, but there are plenty of serious buyers. **Are you open-minded** to listing sooner?

Types + Moments	Objections + Situations	Magic Words
Listing Appointment	I want to wait until I can make a few repairs to the home	Most people want their house to be HGTV ready before they list. But **how would you feel if** the repairs you want to make don't result in any additional profit?
Listing Appointment	I think that your suggested price is too low	**Help me understand** your experience with pricing homes.
Listing Appointment	My home is better than the comp(s) you used and deserves a higher price	**Just out of curiosity, what makes you say that?**
Listing Appointment	Why shouldn't I just list with the #1 company or agent?	**Just imagine** what it's going to be like to have an agent who treats you like their only client. That's the level of dedication I have to the people I work with and my results reflect that.
Listing Appointment	I'm going to hire a discount broker	**What do you understand** about the different levels of service in real estate?
Servicing	Why haven't we had more offers?	**Don't worry**, it's natural to feel frustrated when you have a lot of showings with no offers. That just means we have to get creative about how we price the home to draw more interest.

Types + Moments	Objections + Situations	Magic Words
Servicing	Suggesting a price reduction	**Would you be open-minded** to reducing your asking price if it could create more interest?
Servicing	I'm not willing to stage my home or make any improvements	If I could show you how staging your home or making improvements could result in a significantly higher profit, then **would you be open** to the idea of discussing it as an option?
Servicing	Did we accept an offer too soon?	**Don't worry**, it's natural to feel that way. **Would it help if** I told you that every seller feels the same when they finally accept an offer to sell their home?
Servicing (buyers)	I want to find the perfect home and I'm willing to wait	**Would you be open-minded** to me making some small suggestions to your search criteria to help you find that perfect home?
Servicing (buyers)	We lost out because we should have offered more	**How open-minded are you** to looking at something that could be perfect but a little over your budget?
Servicing (buyers)	We think we offered too much money	**Don't worry**, most buyers have some remorse after their offer is accepted. It's natural.

Types + Moments	Objections + Situations	Magic Words
Service	Referring deals to your team when you previously serviced the client	**How open-minded would you be** to working with my most experienced buyer's agent who I've personally trained?
Closing	Asking for a review	**Would you be open-minded** to shooting a quick video to share your experience working with me? I know it would help a lot of people just like you.
Closing	Asking for a referral	I'm going to ask you to think of someone who could benefit from my services. **Don't worry!** If you don't know who that person is right now, I'll give you some time to think about it before I check back.
Past Client	Reconnecting after a long period of ignoring the customer	I was thinking of you today and **as I promised** when we worked together, I wanted to reach out to let you know that I'm here whenever you might need advice or an update on what's happening in your local market.
Past Client	Asking if they are going to sell this year	Most people are wondering if now is a good time to sell their home. **Just out of curiosity**, have you given any thoughts to selling yours recently?
Past Client	Promoting market stats	**How important is it** to you to be aware of all the homes that are selling near you?

Types + Moments	Objections + Situations	Magic Words
Past Client	Promoting a new listing you have on the market	**I'm not sure if it's for you**, but there's a beautiful new home that just hit the market that's not going to last. Would you like me to send you the details?
Past Client	Promote a listing you have coming soon to the market	**Who do you know** that might want to get access to a home before it hits the market?
Past Client	Expanding your services	**I'm not sure if it's for you**, but if you're interested in buying an investment property in the future, I can keep you in the loop on any good deals that come on the market.
Past Client	How's the market?	**If** I can find some time to put together a detailed report about your neighborhood, **then** would you take a look at it?

Exactly What Your Marketing Should Say: Magic Words for Social Media, Email + Text Messages

Visit Curaytor.com/Exactly for Free Copy and Paste Templates

Now that you understand how to ask better questions and have better conversations that will lead to better outcomes, you might be wondering if and how these same Magic Words that influence people when selling can also be applied to your marketing. They can! And we already did the heavy lifting for you by turning them into copy and paste templates that you can download for free at Curaytor.com/Exactly.

Most people decide if getting our help with their marketing is right for them by asking themselves three simple questions:

- How important is it that you consistently have listings?
- Would it help if you got a new client today by sending one quick email?
- Could it be possible that improving your lead follow-up and past client communication will help your business?

If you answered very, yes and yes then what happens next is that you open up Curaytor.com/Exactly on your phone or computer right now and get access to Exactly What to Say for Real Estate Agents marketing templates for free.

Just imagine how much better your social media efforts, referral business and conversion rates will be when you use the ideas below...

"I'm Not Sure If It's for You, But"

Considering more than ninety percent of people do not buy or sell a home each year it can feel pretty spammy to send just listed or open house invites by email to your past clients or sphere of influence all the time.

With that in mind we have developed an email template for you to send them instead that uses the "I'm not sure if it's for you, but. . ." Magic Words combined with a coming soon or just listed property to get them to either A) reply immediately and say they are interested or B) send you a referral of someone who is. All without being annoying or aggressive.

"Who Do You Know?"

The real estate industry generates tens of millions of buyer leads each year. But capturing seller leads still eludes most agents. Don't worry though, we've actually developed a way to turn the "Who do you know?" Magic Words into a way to get listing leads both online and through direct mail.

"Open-Minded"

When you have a home on the market that is overpriced, using the "open-minded" Magic Words can make asking the seller for a price reduction a lot easier. As opposed to saying "You should lower your asking price," asking "Would you be open-minded to lowering your asking price?" can get you the desired outcome you want.

Working with clients whose homes are listed can be stressful, as can working with buyers who are taking a long time to make a decision on a home. With that in mind we have developed some situational email templates for you to send that turn "open-minded" messages into a "yes" to your ask.

Plus, for when you close a deal we have also developed a template for getting 5-star reviews.

"Opening-Fact-Question"

Let's face it, calling internet leads and dialing for dollars can be a daunting and challenging job. Using our Opening-Fact-Question framework, we've developed a phone script for you to use any time you hit the phones looking for business.

You can use it when calling buyer leads who are interested in one of your listings.

You can use it to call FSBOS and expired listings.

You can use it when you are following up with seller leads.

You can even use it when you are calling your past clients after the sale to ask for an online review.

"What Is Your Experience?"

Often, when we are prospecting and following up with leads we are showcasing our experiences and asking them how we can help. Makes sense. But why not add asking them about their experiences as an additional angle to reach out with? Getting leads to reply or respond in a timely manner can be very challenging. Making the question about them and not you gives you an additional way to get a conversation going, without it all being about you.

We have worked the "What is your experience?" Magic Words into lead follow-up email campaigns as well as one-to-one email and text message templates you can use in sales.

"How Important Is It?"

One of the nice things about having experience is that you can then anticipate what your FAQ (frequently asked questions) will be each time you work with a new buyer or seller. Don't all buyers end up asking about the same questions anyway? Haven't most of the listing appointments you've gone on led to similar questions being asked, or issues of importance to them having been established?

Knowing what they will ask in advance sets you up perfectly to use the "How important is it?" Magic Words when they do. We've identified these FAQs for you and created emails, text messages and phone scripts you can use when they inevitably come up.

"What Do You Understand?"

Let's face it, real estate has become in many ways a Zillow-first experience. Buyers go there first, before they drive around looking for lawn signs or open houses or request a showing. Sellers go there first to see how much their home is worth before they reach out to an agent for a CMA (comparative market analysis, or "comps"). And both buyers and sellers go there to see how well (or poorly) you are doing your job by looking at your 5-star reviews (or lack thereof), before they contact you.

Now when Zillow comes up you can use the "What do you understand about. . ." Magic Words to "win" these "arguments." We have put together a "Tell me what you understand about the Zestimate. . ." library of resources so that you can show them, not just tell them, how the Zestimate really works and why getting a CMA from you is critical if they are serious about selling soon.

In fact, we have an email that you can send to all of your past clients that will fill up your inbox with requests for you to give them an accurate and expert home valuation.

"How Would You Feel If?"

Buying or selling a home is often and justly referred to as an "emotional decision" so it shouldn't surprise you that the "How would you feel if?" Magic Words can help you win more business right away.

We've created a cheat sheet for you of the best questions to ask at a listing appointment or when meeting with a buyer for the first time so that you start with emotion, not logic, when persuading them to work with you. We even categorized them based on loss (which motivates more people) and gain (which also motivates many people).

"Just Imagine"

Picturing oneself buying a home is already a very exciting and appealing idea. Yet most MLS descriptions and ads for listings don't tap into that emotional moment someone is going through. They are so focused on the home itself that they forget that the buyer needs to "see" themselves living in it before they are going to ask you to go see it in person.

Using the Magic Words "Just imagine. . ." we have crafted some compelling copy for your listing promotions that will help them stand out by attracting buyers who are serious about the home because we have already gotten them to "move in" in their mind.

"How Certain Are You?"

Objections are a part of life for any salesperson. Even the most successful real estate agents get a lot of objections. It is often their ability to overcome them without burning bridges that leads to them becoming a top producer. Whether it is over the phone, at a listing presentation or through an email or DM, we've turned the "How certain are you?" Magic Words into a way to handle and overcome the most common and difficult objections agents face.

Because these objections often come at the critical moment of a sales pitch when money is on the line, you will want to keep them handy and start using them right away. I mean, how certain are you that how you are handling objections now is better than our way?

"Could It Be Possible?"

One of the most fascinating parts of the real estate business is that most agents love working with their clients, but they don't always love working with each other. There is a tightrope one must walk when speaking negatively about another agent (even if they actually deserve it.)

Whether you are competing for a listing or you are working with an agent who is difficult to communicate with, using the "Could it be possible?" Magic Words can give you the ability to make your point without being a jerk. After all, you might have to work with or compete against the same agent again and your reputation is everything. We have created some scripts and templates for you that take advantage of "Could it be possible?" so you can make your point without burning bridges.

"Help Me Understand"

If you are in sales you will get objections. It is part of the gig. Your ability to identify them and overcome them, without being pushy, is paramount to having a successful career. Thankfully, the objections we get are typically the same and so our ability to anticipate what they will be and then use the "Help me understand" Magic Words to overcome them is easier than you might think.

If you need help overcoming objections like "I need to think about it/sleep on it" or "I need to speak to my spouse first" or "The other agent/service costs less" or "I am just going to rent for another year," we've got your back.

"When Would Be a Good Time?"

Dealing with rejection is a way of life in sales. Thankfully, now that you are learning exactly what to say and using our Magic Words, you won't be getting rejected nearly as often. That said, you will still get a lot of no's. When you do, take advantage of the "When would be a good time?" Magic Words to confirm another appointment, albeit down the road.

Think of the people who are ready to buy or sell now as helping your checking account and the "When would be a good time?" follow-up appointments as adding to your savings account. In *The Conversion Code,* the acronym PAO (preferred additional outcomes) means that when you get a no, the next goal is a call back the next day, then the next week, then the next month, then email follow up.

By planning for the no's and having these alternate yes's ready you can create a plethora of opportunities down the road. Whether you get rejected in a message or over the phone, we've got your back with situational templates that will get you another swing, even when you swing and miss.

"I'm Guessing You Haven't Gotten Around To"

One of the worst feelings in sales is when you have made your pitch and now the lead is ghosting you. It is one of the more awkward calls to make or messages to send. There is an art to appearing confident when your confidence is indeed wavering.

By using the Magic Words "I'm guessing you haven't gotten around to. . ." when you are following up after an appointment it disarms the lead and creates an environment where they feel comfortable answering, whether that is to deny you or confirm they want to hire you. When you can't get them on the phone or face to face, we have your back. Take advantage of our email and text message templates to turn a lead that is ignoring you into a client who is hiring you.

"You Have Three Options"

Yes, coffee's for closers. But the truth is that no one wants to be "closed." Whether it is an FSBO, an expired listing, a renter, a seller or a buyer, eventually you have to ask for the business. We've turned the "You have three options. . ." Magic Words into a closing talk track for each and all of the aforementioned scenarios. Getting someone's commitment to work with you is your job. And with these simple scripts we just made your job much easier.

"Two Types of People"

At the end of the day there are only two types of people you are going to interact with. Those who are going to buy or sell a home soon and those who are not. Being able to segment your database in a way to focus on those who will transact soon is half the battle. Like one of the top agents in New Jersey, Sue Adler, once told me, "I love talking to people. I just love talking to the ones who are buying or selling a home soon more."

We have turned the "Two types of people" Magic Words into short and sweet emails you can send your list that will quickly identify who is worth focusing on right now versus who is going to hire you later.

"I Bet You're a Bit Like Me"

One of the fastest ways to make a sale is to build trust. One of the fastest ways to build trust is to find common ground. By using the Magic Words "I bet you're a bit like me" you can instantly get a lead or prospect to know that the two of you are on the same page.

These Magic Words also have a captivating, "Once upon a time" quality. It feels like you are reading or listening to a story, not a sales pitch. This can extend a conversation with a new lead over the phone as well as increase the time spent in an email you send or on a blog post you write.

"If. . . Then"

Focusing on the right people in your database is half the battle. In fact, the majority of the ROI in email marketing comes from emails that are sent to a small and relevant segment, not your entire list. The same is true for salespeople. Having them call all the leads is not nearly as effective as calling the ones who want to be called and are actually going to be transacting soon. In Chris' bestseller *The Conversion Code,* he calls this BBF (behavior-based follow-up) being better than simply TBF (time-based follow-up).

We have built you a list of the segments you should create to send emails to, and the segments you should build for your sales team or yourself so that your follow-up hits the bull's-eye while others spray and pray (and fail).

"Would It Help If?"

Let me guess, you have worked with someone who was on the fence about moving forward, but one of the following three things kept them from saying "yes": 1) they needed to wait and think about it; 2) they wanted to talk it over with their spouse before deciding; 3) they wanted to interview at least one more agent before signing.

Sometimes you have to help people across the finish line. Bend their arm, but don't break it. The Magic Words "Would it help if?" are built to get from a "maybe" to a "yes" in those exact moments. So, we have created situational scripts, text messages and email templates for you to use that will turn objections and tough questions from people on the fence into closings and more clients.

"Don't Worry"

Mastering conversations includes the hard ones. When the pressure is on you must rise to the occasion. Plus, be confident in your delivery and certain about your plan of action. Buyers and sellers who you are actively working with each have their own FAQs when things get difficult. We have listed out the ten most common scenarios where a buyer or seller would be most upset and have created a script to guide you to answering each and every one with confidence. All starting with the simple Magic Words, "Don't worry."

"Most People"

If most of the people you work with love their experience, don't be like most people and only collect 5-star reviews. Have a strategy to get the most out of them. We have turned the "Most people" Magic Words into a template you can use to better showcase your positive client feedback as new and effective marketing pieces for your website, social media and across the internet.

"The Good News"

Delivering bad news requires a delicate touch. Positivity wins. That can be a hard mindset to keep when the going gets tough. The good news is we have turned "The good news" Magic Words into cup-half-full bearers of bad news. The next time you have to call or message someone to tell them that things are not going well, these Magic Words and templates will make giving that news sting a lot less and keep a deal from falling apart.

"What Happens Next"

Most agents only work with two types of people, buyers and sellers. We spend so much time trying to convince them to work with us that we often forget to simply explain exactly "What happens next." Doing this paints a picture of what is going to happen the second they stop being a lead and start being a client.

Because this is happening at the moment of truth when they are deciding to work with you or not, you don't want to guess what to say. Money is on the line. So, we have drafted two paragraphs for you (one for buyers and one for sellers) that lay out the next steps and will take you from your pitch to your close, all without missing a beat.

"What Makes You Say That?"

There is a science to sales. When you get denied in person it hurts. But it also hurts to get an objection or rejection in an email, social media DM or text message. As opposed to replying to their concerns with several paragraphs of explanation and supporting examples, next time simply reply with the Magic Words "What makes you say that?" so they will go deeper, expose if they have an objection (or a buying question) and give you a clear path to winning them over.

"Before You Make Up Your Mind"

You will get rejected by internet leads through an email or text at a much higher rate than over the phone or in person. When you do get a "no" or an "I'm not interested" in a message, we have a response ready for you that uses the Magic Words "Before you make up your mind. . ." This will give you one last chance at "saving" a deal and more importantly you will feel good knowing you went all out and didn't lose a lead who may have become a customer (and future referral source).

"If I Can, Will You?"

We wanted to have some fun with this phrase and turn it into a bunch of requests for small favors. . .

If I can get you to admit right now that you love this book, then will you leave a 5-star review on Amazon and share a picture of the cover on social media?

If I can make it to the next conference you attend, then will you recommend that they bring me in to host the "Exactly What to Say for Real Estate Agents" workshop?

If I can get you a really fair price per book, then will you buy ten more copies to give away as gifts right now?

If I can help you improve your income through what you learned in this book, then will you email me and let me know that it helped?

If I can get you access to our "Exactly What to Say for Real Estate Agents" online coaching course, then will you head over to Curaytor.com/Exactly now and claim your spot?

If I can send you exactly what to say in your digital marketing and to your leads when you call them every single week, then will you go to Curaytor.com/Book and learn more about hiring us?

"Just One More Thing"

The best time to sell someone something is when they are buying something. A good example of this is how retail stores stock up the areas you stand and wait to check out which inevitably leads you to grab "Just one more thing" while waiting in line.

When you capture a lead online there are also these same "upsell" opportunities with your confirmation messages on your landing pages and in your autoresponders.

"A Favor"

We turned each item below into an email request template that focus on these scenarios:

- Secured a great offer for your client
- Helped a prospect find their dream home
- Negotiated a great compromise
- Introduced a valuable third party
- Ran a successful open house
- Took the time to show someone a new area

"As Promised"

We tend to overcomplicate business. Ultimately, people just want us to make them a promise, then keep it. Yet time and time again we hear horror stories of exactly the opposite. Overpromise, underdeliver even feels like the status quo at times. But you are different. You keep your promises. And as a real estate agent you probably have to get back to people with information, often.

So, we have created a dozen or so "As promised" Magic Word email and text message templates that you can send when you do what you said you would.

"Just Out of Curiosity"

Some of the most talented salespeople of all time have been hung up on, cussed out or had a door slammed in their face. Rejection is part of the profession. So why wouldn't you prepare for it, be ready for when it happens and do something about it? You can't turn every "I want to wait and think about it" objection into a "never mind I want to sign right now," but you can and should try. It is your job to ask for the business. It is their job to reject you. It is your job to ask for the business again.

Nowadays, a lot of rejection and the objections we face in sales actually happen over email, in text messages or on social media. The next time you get a message that says they want to wait, use our "Just out of curiosity" Magic Words that we wrote for you and give yourself another shot at success.

Simple Swaps

If you were to read a thousand MLS descriptions, 999 of them might sound exactly the same. Cute, charming, spacious, cozy, fixer-upper. The words that agents choose to describe the properties they list have become so overused and unchanged that we wanted to do something about it.

With Simple Swaps to your MLS descriptions you can make your copy really pop and stand out when people read it on your website or on popular mobile apps. This can greatly impact the quality and quantity of leads you generate from something you are already doing. Our Magic Words for MLS descriptions are going to help your property stand out and impress your seller at the same time.

Final Thought

With all these words to consider, I am sure you are now aware that reaching for the right words at the right time can make all the difference. Please note that although the words themselves hold immense levels of power, their success in application is also hugely dependent upon your confidence and competence in how and when you use them.

Peter Parker's (aka Spiderman's) Uncle Ben famously said, "With great power comes great responsibility" and given what you have been gifted through this book, that responsibility is granted to you.

My assumption through all my work is that the people I am teaching have high levels of integrity, are acting with their clients' interests ahead of their own and are committed to creating win-win scenarios for all parties.

Becoming a masterful communicator takes, time, effort, heart, practice and a humble energy that is dedicated to progress. Have fun failing and enjoy your journey of progress—do the work to turn my words into your words. This industry is littered with scripts that promise you ten times the success and although scripts certainly have their place, they can sound robotic, lack sincerity and prevent you from having the freedom you need for authentic communication.

Instead, use the lessons in this book to craft your own scripts, in your words, that sound like you and how you communicate and then *learn* your scripts so you can enjoy being fully present in your conversations.

Write them out word for word and periodically refine them based on your own personal experience. There are critical moments that exist at a number of key points in your sales process and being professional enough to craft your conversations ahead of time will mean that you will move from counting conversations to making conversations count.

Everything you have learned in this book is simple, easy to do and, better still, works.

Oh, and one more thing...
Everything you have learned in this book is simple, easy to do and, better still, works.

What it does not do, though, is work with *all* of the people *all* of the time. It just works with *most* of the people *most* of the time. There is a chance that what you are doing now is working with *some* of the people *some* of the time, so please do not try this once and tell me it did not work. Try it over and over again until it becomes natural. Bring it into everyday language and practice in areas of your life outside of your real estate business. The compound effect of those tiny improvements and subtle changes in language will soon mean that in the situations where it matters most you will know exactly what to say, when to say it and how to make it count.

I wish you all the success that you are prepared to work for. Please enjoy the journey.

Acknowledgments

Following the launch of the original version of my "little book," *Exactly What to Say* has rapidly become a major part of my world and something that I become increasingly more proud of and even more protective of every day.

The idea to extend the reach of my "Magic Words" and work with specific industries had always intrigued me, but I knew to do it "right" it was essential to find the perfect partner and share the writing and editorial lens with someone who could really support the expertise of the reader.

Better than a single person, I had the privilege of partnering with two passionate, committed and very talented individuals. Working with Chris, Jimmy and the entire Curaytor team has been a joy, and the combined efforts toward crafting a tool that really helps the real estate industry has been something for which I am eternally grateful.

To help dig deep into the realities of the world as an agent, it was imperative to work with people who are living this as their reality day in and day out.

A huge personal thank-you to all of the agents who braved the New England winter to join us for much of the research in crafting this edition and testing the material in this book and Field Guide. Your essential input really helped shape this book. In particular, thanks goes to:

Amy Foley, Carrie Scoville and Jodi Shea of the Scoville Foley Team

Eric Rollo of Eric Rollo Real Estate Team

Ilya Rasner of The Rasner Group

Lisa Sevajian of The Boston Property Shop/Compass

Stewart Woodward of The Metrowest Home Team

Susana Murphy of ALANTE Real Estate

Further thanks goes to my ever-patient and insanely productive publishing partners at Page Two. Specific attention needs to be pointed to Trena White, for her insane trust in me and strength in leadership; Peter Cocking and Taysia Louie, for doing the work again and again to finalize and shape the cover concept created by Mike Mangigian; and Gabrielle Narsted, for more reasons than there are words to give thanks in the dictionary!

A final thanks goes to you, yes *you*, reading these words right now. We worked as hard as we did on this for you and your benefit. The fact that you made it to this point in the book gives me every confidence that our combined efforts will be more than worth it.

Change your *words*, and you can change our *world*.

About the Authors

Chris Smith and Jimmy Mackin are the co-founders of Curaytor. They help real estate agents, teams and brokerages increase the ROI of their marketing and improve their lead conversion rates using technology, content and coaching. Their work has been featured in *Adweek, Forbes, Entrepreneur, Fortune* and the *Huffington Post*. Curaytor was also recently named one of *Inc.* magazine's 500 Fastest-Growing Companies in America.

Chris and Jimmy have spoken at hundreds of events including conferences hosted by HubSpot, the National Association of REALTORS® and Inman News. Chris was named one of the American Marketing Association's Four Under 40 Emerging Leaders, and his book *The Conversion Code* is a *USA Today* bestseller that has been translated into six different languages.

Contact them directly at Chris@Curaytor.com or Jimmy@Curaytor.com.

Phil M. Jones is a serial entrepreneur, business growth expert and the bestselling author of *Exactly What To Say*, *Exactly How To Sell*, and *Exactly Where To Start*. He had his first business at just fourteen years of age and is the youngest recipient of the British Excellence in Sales and Marketing award.

To date, over two million people across fifty-seven countries have benefited from Phil's lessons and, as a result, they now know exactly what to say, when to say it and how to make more of their conversations count.

Learn more about Phil at www.philmjones.com.

A Shameless Plug

My guess is that if you have got this far in the book, then you must have found at least part of it valuable to you and your personal success. Modern books are now judged using the universal recognition of an Amazon review. I'm not sure if it's for you, but would it be okay for you to take a few seconds and help us to create the most reviewed book in the real estate industry?

Also, know that the team at Curaytor are *very* active on social media and if you want to share your opinions of the book online, then be sure to include me and my co-authors in your posts and add to our hashtag #exactlywhattosay.

@philmjonesuk
@Chris_Smth
@jimmymackin
@curaytorsystems

While I'm asking, I guess it would make sense to let you know how else we might be able to help each other.

Because I am smart enough to own all my publishing rights, my team and I can help you directly with bulk orders of this book and save you a fortune. We can also change the cover to suit your brokerage or brand and may even be open to changing the examples and foreword to support your personal goals. This customization is a service I perform for many of my speaking clients, and I would love the opportunity to discuss doing the same for you. Please email Bonnie at speaking@philmjones.com and learn more about how *Exactly What to Say* can help you to build your brand.